Win-Win
Selling

Turning Customer **NEEDS** into **SALES**

How to order: single copies may be ordered online at www.novavistapub.com.

ISBN 978-90-77256-34-3

D/2011/9797/1

Printed in the United States of America

20 19 18 17 16 15 14 13 12

Cover design: Wouter Geukens
Text design: Layout Sticker

Contents

Foreword by Larry Wilson 8

1. **Loving Your Job: the Counselor Mindset** 11
   Performance with Fulfillment 12
   Help the Buyer Win – A Story of Evolution 13
      The Counselor Evolution 16
   How the Counselor Approach Works 18
      The Four Obstacles to Buying 18
      Relating: Dealing with No Trust 19
      Discovering: Dealing with No Need 19
      Advocating: Dealing with No Help 20
      Supporting: Dealing with No Satisfaction 20
      Counselor Selling in Action 20
   A True Win-Win Solution 21

2. **Relating Skills: The Key to Overcoming Trust Resistance** 22
   Time, Tension, and Trust 23
   Close the Credibility Gap 25
      Propriety 26
      Competence 27
      Commonality 28
      Intent 30
   Prove Your Good Intentions with the 3 Ps 32
   Build Empathy by Emulating Ben Duffy 33
   An Action Plan for Improving Relating Skills 35

3. **Discovering the Discovery Process** 37
   Discovering in the Counselor Selling Era 37

Tweaking the Golden Rule 39

Shining a Light on Unseen Needs 42

Digging Into the Gap: The Discovery Agreement 43

Discovery's Vital Engine: The Art of Questioning 45

Two Ears, One Mouth: The Value of Listening Well 50

Don't Overlook Purchase Influencers in Discovery 52

Avoid These Discovery Faux Pas 54

Why They Buy: Identifying Task and Personal Motives 56

And Now, for the Weather Report 60

4. **Advocating, Presenting and Closing** 63

   Section 1: THE BASICS OF ADVOCATING 63

      Balancing the Bicycle 65

      Avoiding Irrelevance 67

      The SAB Alternative 70

      The Dangers of Fast-Forwarding Through Discovery 72

   Section 2: THE ART OF THE SALES PRESENTATION 74

      Adapting Your Advocating Strategy to Role Players 76

      Winning the Day Before the Day 80

      Gathering Competitive Intelligence 83

      How "Word Laziness" Can Cost You Sales 84

      The Third-Party Story: The Ultimate Illustrator 87

      Ingredients of Good Third-Party Stories 88

   Section 3: HANDLING OBJECTIONS AND CLOSING 90

      Using the Assumptive Close 91

      Managing Your Fears about Closing 94

      The LSCPA Model: Understanding Objections to Death 96

      Handling the Complex Objection 102

      Appealing to the Buyer's Task Agenda 103

      Appealing to the Personal Motives 106

5. Supporting Skills **112**

The "No Hurry" Phenomenon 113

The Zone of Indifference 114

Helping vs. Controlling: The Four Pillars of Support 116

    The First Pillar: Supporting the Buying Decision 117

    The Second Pillar: Managing the Implementation 120

    The Third Pillar: Proactively Handling Dissatisfaction 121

    The Fourth Pillar: Enhancing the Relationship 125

Adding Value Through Expertise and Networking 128

6. Counselor Selling in Action **130**

Your Client is Just Comparing Prices 130

Your Client Takes the Job Inside 133

Your Non-Profit Rates Look Too Low 135

You Run into Gatekeepers 137

Your Client's Budget Suddenly Gets Cut 139

Your Company May Be Bought Soon 142

Your Client Buys Through a Purchasing Committee 144

Your Client is Setting Up Preferred Providers 146

Your Client's CEO Awards the Deal to a Friend 147

You Sell in a Declining Industry 149

You Sell for the First Time in a New Culture 151

Resources 154

Contributors 156

Index 158

Foreword

The publication of this book is a fulfilling moment for me, since it extends the benefits of the Counselor selling approach to many readers. It also takes me back to my earliest days in sales, in the Fifties. I was earning $200 and spending $210 each month, teaching high school. My uncle recruited me into the life insurance business, promising I would make $400 per month. I actually believed I would never have another financial challenge in my lifetime.

It wasn't easy at first. I was shocked that some people didn't want to talk to me as a life insurance agent. I started reading Victor Frankel's book, *Man's Search for Meaning*. It helped me weather the emotional slings and arrows of outrageous rejection. Frankel's message about the final freedom that everyone experiences when faced with any adversity encouraged me as if he were whispering right into my psyche.

For my seven years in the business I stayed at the top of my company's sales success chart and became the Youngest Lifetime Member of the Million Dollar Roundtable. That honor led to invitations to speak at meetings and share my selling secrets. I accepted them, even though I couldn't articulate what my secrets actually were. So I borrowed other people's secrets and spoke articulately as though they were mine.

Then the unexpected happened. A client company to whom I had presented my secrets-of-somebody-else's-success speech asked if I would create a training program for them. My immediate, fearful thought was, "I don't know how to do that," but nonetheless, I said yes.

Then it occurred to me. Until the Sixties, selling was seen as an adversarial relationship – the seller beats the buyer in a win-lose scenario. You heard about 110 ways to close a sale, 88 ways to answer an objection. This clearly wasn't the basis of *my* success. So I went looking for my own secrets. I lucked out when I paid $1.00 for a psychology book. The only part I read was by Brandice University's head of psychology, Abraham Maslow, defining his pyramid of needs. I had never heard of him, even though he pioneered in humanistic psychology.

I soon met with Dr. Maslow because I knew his concepts had something to do with my "humanistic" view of selling. It was a defining moment. Maslow guided me to Dr. Carl Rogers, a well-known therapist, who authored *On Becoming a Person* and *Client-Centered Therapy*. These books, combined with Maslow's humanistic perspective, became the soil in which the Counselor concept began to germinate and provide the harvest for an entirely new mindset on selling.

Dr. Rogers helped me understand the model of counseling, which is an integrated philosophy, discipline, and set of skills. These help the client solve problems, find advantages, and reap the benefits of new solutions. Applied to selling, the *Counselor* salesperson benefits by creating a win-win relationship and a loyal customer.

Helping people get what they want and feel the way they want to feel was what I couldn't express earlier. Essentially the model says, "The more I help *others* get what they want, the more I get what I want." This new model felt right, and helped me discover and become more of my true self – the person I was when I was at my best.

I don't know how many millions of people have been through the Counselor Salesperson program offered by Wilson Learning since 1965. But I do know that those who have absorbed its full message have discovered the power of its secrets not only in their work lives, but more importantly, in *all* aspects of their lives. In learning to counsel with their clients, they also learn to counsel within their most important relationships – with family, friends, themselves.

I started Wilson Learning with a purpose statement that was inspired by Dr. Maslow – "helping others become as much as they can be." I hope, as you read this book, you can combine your life purpose with these powerful competencies. Counsel yourself to become as much as *you* can be, while counseling your clients to become as much as *they* can be. You'll both enjoy the ultimate win-win. I wish you all the best.

Larry Wilson

The Counselor Mindset

4 Supporting completes the cycle, ensuring customers experience the benefits of solutions and see needs met. Reinforces your Counselor role in the implementation; reveals the next problems to solve together. Avoids dissatisfaction; gives you a sustainable advantage.

1 Relating creates an open, trusting relationship with your customers and enhances your credibility. Lays the groundwork for genuine problem solving. Demonstrates good intent. Avoids problems stemming from customers' initial tension about your intent and ability to help.

Supporting · No Satisfaction · Relating · No Trust

Problem Solving Attitude

Advocating · No Help · Discovering · No Need

3 Advocating links the outcomes of Discovery to your offering and engages your customers as partners. Involves customers as internal supporters of your jointly developed solution. Avoids customers' sense that the offer gives no help for their situation.

2 Discovering engages the customers in candidly sharing information so you can together define their needs and problems, the very ones which create the Gap that prevents them from getting to their desired states. Avoids the common perception there's no need to buy.

The Counselor method combines win-win, problem solving attitudes with people skills, in a four-stage cycle. But the whole – the Counselor mindset and the Counselor selling skills – is really greater than the sum of its parts.

1 | Loving Your Job: the Counselor Mindset

Picture this: you love your job in sales, and you are really good at it. You get up each morning excited about the joys and challenges of the day. You know you are doing something that helps other people and makes them feel good about themselves. You solve problems and make things better. Your customers welcome you warmly. You're a successful salesperson, and you feel great.

Unfortunately, that picture doesn't describe every salesperson today. And if you look for books to help you sell better, you find that most people do not believe that salespeople can or should feel good about themselves. Titles like *Guerilla Selling* or *How to Sell Anything to Anyone* create the wrong impression about successful salespeople. How can you feel good about your job day after day if your primary goal is to pull a sale out of your customer's pocket?

At Wilson Learning Worldwide we reject that approach to selling. We believe, and our research shows, that the most successful salespeople gain happiness and fulfillment from being a different kind of salesperson. They reach fulfillment by seeing selling as a way to help customers get what they truly need and want. This philosophy fundamentally changes what happens between the salesperson and the customer. You, the seller, become a counselor for your customer. That is why we call it the Counselor Approach.

With this book, you can master the practical, proven skills of the Counselor Approach and adopt the Counselor Mindset. When you do, you will sell well and feel good about it. At Wilson Learning, we call this *Performance with Fulfillment*. It is a powerful tool, not an impossible dream.

PERFORMANCE WITH FULFILLMENT

Look around at the workers you know – other salespeople, colleagues, friends. You can locate each one somewhere on the Performance with Fulfillment matrix.

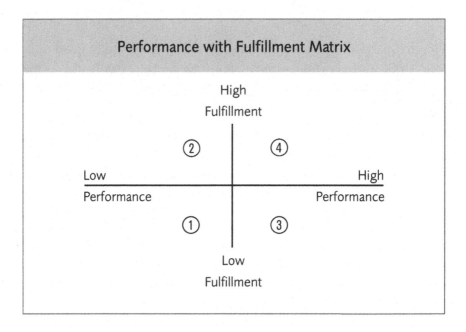

1. **Low Performance – Low Fulfillment**: Hopefully you don't have too many of these people around you, but there always a few. These folks drag themselves into work each day, doing the minimum needed not to get fired. They hate their work, hate their work environment, and, most importantly, don't think that they produce anything of value.

2. **Low Performance – High Fulfillment**: These people are excited by their jobs, love working with their co-workers, and think they are making a difference in the world. Unfortunately, they lack the skills or abilities to actually make it happen. This group includes lots of new hires, thrilled with their jobs but not very good at them – yet.

3. High Performance – Low Fulfillment: You probably also know a few of these folks. If they are salespeople, they make a lot of sales. But how do they achieve their numbers? Do they manipulate or dupe buyers, selling without any consideration for whether their customer needs their product or not? Are they complainers? ("I could make more sales if I had better leads, better products to sell," and so on.) Do they get any repeat business? With little trust or appreciation from their customers, no wonder they aren't happy.

4. High Performance – High Fulfillment: You can't miss these people. They are the highest performing sellers, and they love it. They talk passionately about what it means to serve a customer. They get a kick out of understanding the customer's problem and fashioning a solution that improves the customer's business or life. These salespeople walk away rather than sell a customer a product he doesn't need. Customers love them.

> ## What Drives a Counselor Salesperson?
>
> At a training session in Singapore, we met a dozen insurance salespeople. They sold group life insurance to large multinational corporations. At the end of the first day, after talking about Performance with Fulfillment, we asked the question "What is your job?" Next morning, one of the participants announced that he had spent half the night thinking about this question. This fellow, the highest performing salesperson in the group, said it boiled down to a single sentence: "My job is to make sure that every family in the world feels financially secure." He really knows what Performance with Fulfillment is all about!

HELP THE BUYER WIN – A STORY OF EVOLUTION

To understand how the Counselor Approach is different from other approaches to selling, let's look at the evolution of the practice of selling and buying. The approaches of salespeople and buyers have changed over time, particularly in the ways the sellers regard buyers' needs.

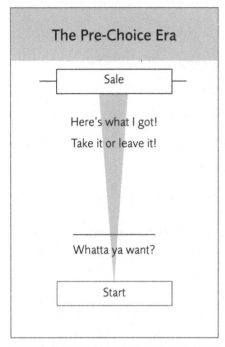

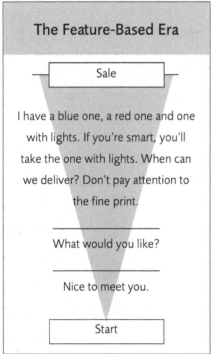

The Pre-Choice Era

In the early days of "selling," new technology and inventions were rare, distribution was limited, and copying or knocking off products wasn't easy. As a result, the seller who put a unique product before the buyer had a clear, sustainable advantage over other sellers. "I'm the only game in town" was often quite true for these storefront vendors. If customers needed the product, they sought out the seller – they had virtually no choice.

The sales approach was "Whatta ya want? Here's what I got! Take it or leave it!". Advantage to the *seller*.

The Feature-Based Era

The Pre-Choice Era didn't last long because advances in technology turned local markets into regional and then global ones. Companies began to produce greater numbers of products and to transport them over greater distances. The number of vendors and sources for goods increased. Competition among vendors heated up. As a result, buyers found more options for purchasing goods and services, and prices started falling. The score changed, and it was advantage to the *buyer* – sort of.

Sellers retreated at first and resorted to trickery – "selling strategies" like bait and switch, loss leaders, fine print clauses in contracts, and so forth. Then they tried to differentiate their products based on "features." The bells and whistles added in this era ranged from decorative to valuable – valuable to someone, but not everyone. So the approach to selling became: "What would you like? I've got a blue one, a red one, and one with lights. If you're smart, you'll take the one with lights. I'll let you pay on the installment plan (but don't read the fine print). When can we deliver?"

Sellers regained the advantage, but soon most of them were offering the same features. Low prices became the next point of differentiation, and a lot of businesses went bankrupt as profits shrank.

The Needs-Based Era

Then a major paradigm shift occurred between buyers and sellers. Sellers realized that, if they could not have a product, feature, or price advantage, perhaps they could differentiate themselves by the way they sold. The concept of needs-based selling goes like this: "Instead of adding features to our products to make them serve the widest possible use, let's identify the features that we can produce best and cheapest, then identify the buyers who most want those features and sell to them."

Sellers left their storefronts

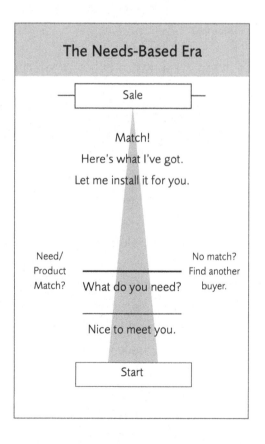

and started reaching out, targeting buyers. Instead of saying, "You need this," salespeople started asking, "Do you need this?" If the buyer needed it, they made a sale. If the buyer didn't, they just moved on to the next buyer. The seller stopped wasting time, energy, and money trying to force the product down the throat of the buyer who really didn't want what was being sold. The approach became, "What do you need?

1. I have what you need – when can we deliver? Or,
2. I'll call back in two months to see if your needs have changed."

Both the seller and buyer gained some advantage here. Sellers were less pushy in their selling and had better odds of success, and buyers faced less pressure to buy and got better service. But the seller was still *selling*.

THE COUNSELOR EVOLUTION

Many companies still use this needs-based sales approach and use it effectively. But about 40 years ago a new approach, a sub-species of the needs-based approach, began to emerge. In the United States, Larry Wilson, founder of Wilson Learning, labeled this new creature the Counselor salesperson. Three distinct traits set this approach apart from the basic needs-based approach.

1. Counselor salespeople don't see themselves primarily as salespeople. They see themselves primarily as "Counselors," whose prime responsibility is to *make the client successful through the purchase and implementation of their product or service.*
2. Counselor selling creates a partnership between you and the buyer. You don't match buyers' needs to your product. Instead, you work with customers to identify the best solutions for their problems.
3. After the sale, the Counselor stays by the customer's side to ensure that the solution works to the customer's satisfaction.

As a result of these critically important traits, the Counselor stops selling and, instead, "counsels" with the buyer, who in turn becomes the client or even the patient.

The Counselor starts by building trust with the client, and then continues with the needs-based era's process of defining needs – except that now the Counselor asks, "What are your business problems?" not "What do you need?" The focus now is buyer-centered, not seller-centered. The buyer's answer lets the Counselor determine whether he or she can help or not. If it's *yes*, then the reply is, "I'd like to suggest that we work together to adapt our brand offering to make it work for you." If it's *no*, then, "I'd like to call back in a month or so to see if your problems have changed."

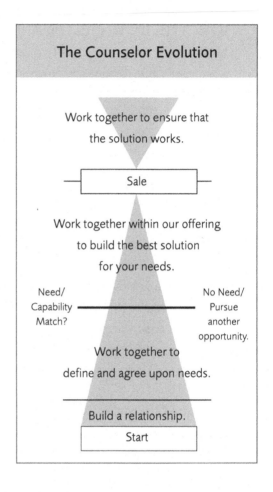

Clearly, this Counselor Approach makes for a significant advantage to the customer, because problems get solved. It's also a significant advantage for the seller and his or her organization, because the counseling skills of the sales team become a unique, strategic advantage that the competition cannot replicate. When the Counselor Approach is followed successfully, the customer sees the relationship with the selling organization as a business partnership, one that is very hard for the competition to displace. The costs of switching simply become prohibitive.

HOW THE COUNSELOR APPROACH WORKS

The Counselor approach has two aspects, which work together to increase your value to your customer and enhance your sales performance:

- The Counselor Selling Skills, and
- The Counselor Mindset.

The other chapters of this book will provide you with the skills of a Counselor salesperson. But before learning the skills, it is important to understand how they work together. While using the skills independently will improve your sales performance, understanding and using them with the Counselor Mindset will significantly enhance their impact. The whole is really greater than the sum of the parts.

The Counselor Mindset starts with this assumption: *People love to buy but hate to be sold*. People are happier when they feel that they have made a reasonable and conscious decision to choose one option over all the others available.

The Four Obstacles to Buying

Recently, Helga set out to buy a digital camera for a client's project. She returned a few hours later, disappointed and without a camera. The reasons why she didn't buy provide a good example of the major barriers that a Counselor salesperson needs to anticipate and address.

1. *No Trust.* "I kept getting conflicting information about the cameras. No one seemed to really know what they were talking about."
2. *No Need.* "They didn't listen to me. I tried to explain what I needed to do with the camera but all they did was talk about pixels and stuff I didn't want to know about."
3. *No Help.* "They just said 'this is the best camera' without explaining why it was the best one for me."
4. *No Satisfaction.* "In the end I felt pressured and manipulated. I never want to go in that camera store again."

The Counselor salesperson understands that these four obstacles to buying are present in every potential customer. Counselor selling provides a systematic approach that helps the salesperson address and avoid each obstacle in turn. Chapters 2 through 5 cover these topics.

Relating: Dealing with No Trust

People will not buy from sellers they believe do not have the buyer's best interests in mind. Nor will customers willingly share important information about their problems, needs, or goals unless they believe that the salesperson has the intent and ability to help them.

Chapter 2 shows how a Counselor salesperson creates an open, trusting relationship with a customer. The Relating skills in Chapter 2 will help you to establish credibility, build trust, and lay the groundwork for a problem-solving sales relationship with your customers. As a result, you will quickly be able to reduce the tension that is normal to any sales relationship and build the bond that will help you help your customers.

Discovering: Dealing with No Need

Bob was remodeling his kitchen and knew he needed a new floor. But beyond that, Bob didn't really know what kind of floor he needed. What Bob knew best were his *problems*. He knew his legs got tired from standing on the old, hard ceramic tiles; he knew that his kids spilled a lot and that the dogs tracked in muddy footprints all the time.

What customers know best are *their* problems, goals, and visions for the future. A Counselor salesperson uses Discovery skills to understand these things, and then goes on to work with the customer to dig deeper, prioritize, and group them into an organized set of needs.

Thus, for the Counselor salesperson, Discovery goes beyond the needs-based stage of asking, "What do you need? Let me see if I have a product to match." Instead, Discovering needs is a process that says, "Let's understand your problems, goals, and priorities. Because then together, we can discover what is most important to you."

Advocating: Dealing with No Help

You've been there. You spent some time with a salesperson; you think he or she listened to you as you described your situation and needs. You wait for his or her response and out comes a canned presentation, detailing features and benefits. You don't have a clue about whether they will solve your problem. This might be the right solution, but there is no way of knowing, given the presentation.

Advocating, addressed in detail in Chapter 4, is not about how to give a good "presentation," but about how to link the Discovery of the customer's needs to the characteristics of your solution. Advocating skills help you make your customer a partner in the presentation of the solution. Thus, Advocating is less about "This is the solution I (the salesperson) recommend" and more about "Here is the solution we built together." This is especially important when there are multiple buyers with different motivations and needs. The Advocating step gives you an internal champion that will help you sell to others in the buyer's organization, others who may have different buying motives.

Supporting: Dealing with No Satisfaction

Counselor salespeople never lose a sale because of "buyer's remorse." Why? Because they recognize that the sale never really ends until the customer has experienced the benefits of the product or service and is satisfied that the critical needs are met. So they follow up on implementation, troubleshoot, adjust, and listen hard for clues about new problems and needs that could lead to future work together.

Chapter 5 provides you with skills for dealing proactively with potential sources of dissatisfaction. It shows how to assure the four critical Support needs (support for the decision, implementation, objections, and the relationship) are addressed.

Counselor Selling in Action

The last chapter of this book gives you some real-life lessons about how the Counselor Approach works in a variety of circumstances. You will find the cases helpful in seeing how the rich resources of the Counselor skills and the Counselor Mindset come together to solve customers' problems, meet challenges from new circumstances, and more. Finally, the section on Other Resources which follows Chapter 6 will lead you to additional sources of information and training in this approach.

A TRUE WIN-WIN SOLUTION

The Counselor Approach creates a true win-win solution, with genuine advantage for both the customer and the salesperson. Customers gain advantage because they get what they need and want without extra features that don't provide any value but that do add cost. Counselor salespeople also gain advantage because they end up creating a trusting relationship with customers that the competition cannot easily replicate or compete with effectively. When the Counselor Approach is implemented successfully, the customer sees the relationship with the selling organization as a business partnership, one he or she values and wants to continue.

While this book cannot replace the live practice and experience that is provided in Wilson Learning's Counselor salesperson workshops, we hope your journey through this book inspires you and helps you gain more fulfillment – and better performance – in your role as a salesperson.

2 | Relating Skills:
The Key to Overcoming
Trust Resistance

"Never trust a salesperson." It's a rule many of us learn early in life. We hear our uncle's story of the used car that fell apart, a sister's tirade about the laptop computer that falls far short of promised performance, or dad's frustration with the industrial machinery salesperson who's never set foot inside a production plant. Those lessons transfer to our own buying experiences. We're quick to project the unseemly tactics of one salesperson to all salespeople, painting them all with the same broad brush.

As salespeople, we've seen this ingrained skepticism ruin good prospects for no apparent reason. We've thoroughly researched a prospective client's company and industry. We've met with contacts inside the company and, through diligent work, devised a winning sales approach. We can prove that we can save the prospect time, money, and effort – or perhaps meet some powerful emotional need – because we have the right product or service at the right price. The prospect agrees that our solution could be right. But still he or she doesn't buy.

Why? Because the prospect doesn't trust us. We are, after all, sales-people.

TIME, TENSION, AND TRUST

Yet every one of us is born with the skills to build trust in people. We've avoided the barrier of distrust in all sorts of situations: when we first move into a new neighborhood and make friends with the neighbors, when we begin dating, when we're hired for a new job. Most of us have plenty of people who trust us in our personal lives. So why is it so hard in a sales relationship?

It isn't, but we often make it so. The problem is we speed through the trust-building stage to get to the transaction – to the end game of making the sale – so we can move on to the next and the next. But think about it. Did your spouse fully trust you on the first date? Did your neighbors let you baby-sit their newborn your first day in the neighborhood? Did your boss reveal all the company secrets during your orientation? Probably not. Yet too often we expect that level of trust from prospects in the formative stage of a relationship.

It's natural to distrust someone in the beginning of any relationship; there's tension because we aren't yet comfortable with the person. People will distrust you for no other reason than you're an unknown commodity or because they're accustomed to dealing with another salesperson. This is called *relationship tension*. This lack of trust is seldom verbalized, but can be picked up through certain behavioral clues. For instance, a prospect feeling no trust might appear:

- Hurried or unwilling to give you much time.
- Preoccupied with other, "more pressing" tasks.
- Uncomfortable or anxious, avoiding direct eye contact.
- Cagey or unwilling to share serious or full information. Prospects provide the barest of data in response to questions, and no attempt is made to "fill in" or "round out" answers in order to give you a better understanding of nuances. The prospect may not feel it's

worth the time to educate someone he or she isn't going to do business with anyway.

The good news is that these defensive responses are normal and to be expected. The fact that there's little trust at this stage of the relationship doesn't necessarily imply a prospect has a negative opinion of you. What it does mean is the prospect doesn't yet know enough about you to determine whether you deserve his confidence – he or she simply needs more information. Relationship tension naturally diminishes over time as we get to know and trust someone.

In a sales situation, where buyer and seller are both motivated to get a job done, there's also *task tension*. It's the tension both sides feel to get on with a job or task, or to work together toward a shared goal. Task tension is usually low during the feeling-out period of a sales negotiation, then builds steam as duties or deadlines are defined, and signs of progress – results – are expected.

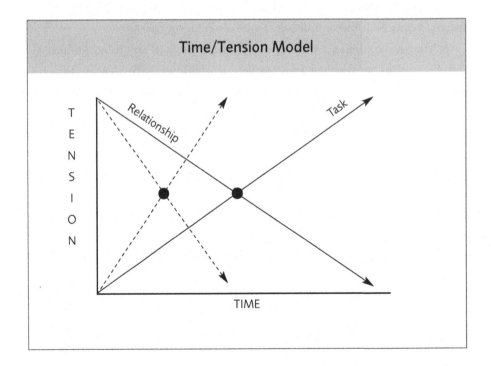

In the early stages of a business relationship, however, the prospect isn't necessarily motivated to get the job done by working with *you* – often because there's a trust issue (relationship tension). Some additional signals that relationship tension is high and task tension is low include a prospect:

- Cutting a meeting short
- Discussing only low-priority issues
- Not providing sufficient information that could help define a sales solution

Your goal, then, is clear: to reduce relationship tension and increase task tension at a faster clip. How? Through the proven Relating skills described in this chapter. The earlier in the relationship the client trusts you, the earlier you can begin a serious discussion of business opportunities.

CLOSE THE CREDIBILITY GAP

The time it takes to establish trust largely depends on the client. A number of factors enter into his or her decision to trust: the nature of the client's past experiences with salespeople, the industry, complexity or size of the sale, your own personality, and other factors. Many salespeople are content to let "nature take its course," believing that through the course of general conversation prospects will come to see they're "okay" people and start to build trust. But there are problems with this approach, not the least of which is it could take a long time – more than the prospect has available – and its haphazard nature may leave a lot of the prospect's questions unanswered. Far better to have a plan for establishing credibility as quickly as possible.

Research from Wilson Learning Worldwide has identified four key building blocks of credibility, traits that, when combined, can quickly allay any trust issues customers may have. They are propriety, competency, commonality and intent.

Proper May Not Be Fancy

Patrick was hired as a livestock feed sales-person. He had a degree in animal nutrition, made it through sales training with flying colors, and appeared to have a real knack for the job. Yet he was fired within two months. "He would wear an expensive suit and tie to the farms, even after we suggested he not," says his sales manager. "He thought he could impress the farmers with a professional look. He didn't understand they wanted someone who dressed like they did on a non-work day: nice slacks and shirts but nothing flashy." Patrick's sales technique also proved a bit too transparent. He thought his degree gave him the credibility to use farming jargon freely, yet his overuse of lingo appeared forced and inappropriate. Seems his farmer-prospects just wanted him to know his stuff – and be real.

Propriety

This is the "hygiene factor" in sales. It gets you in the game – the table stakes – yet it's rarely sufficient to beat the competition and land the big pot. Propriety means behaving appropriately for the customer's business and calibrating your behavior to their expectations. It includes appropriate dress (looking the part), good manners, using the correct protocol and speaking appropriately. In short, it shows that you value and respect what your customers do.

If you're just starting to sell in a new industry – one with traditions, expectations, or protocols unfamiliar to you – there are a few ways to cover yourself on propriety issues.

- Find a mentor. Someone who has sold in the industry for several years can clue you in on what to wear, how to greet people, and how casual your language can be. If need be, role-play with him or her and ask for a critique on your approach.
- Live among your customers. Ask if you can spend a day shadowing people in jobs representative of those you'll be selling to, or schedule less-intrusive informational phone calls to pick customers' brains on current issues or trends in the industry.

- Attend an industry convention. Don't attend as a salesperson, but as a sleuth. Be a fly on the wall. Watch how interactions are conducted and how others comport themselves. Spend some time questioning vendors in the exhibit area. You'll not only learn about appropriate behavior for the industry, you'll be briefed on the latest buzz.

Competence

Simply put, customers want to know you can do the job and that you know their business almost as well as they do. They want to know you've succeeded before and will have little trouble replicating – or exceeding – the feat. You may be a wonder of propriety and a paragon of good intentions, but if prospects feel you don't have the knowledge or skills to solve their problems, you're out of luck.

To demonstrate competence in the early stage of a relationship, consider:

- Mentioning your background, training, or industry experience in a a conversation without making a "Story of Me" presentation. Some salespeople hesitate to do this because they don't want to be in the position of "telling" at the start of an interview, but the fact is buyers expect this sort of information.
- Responding to a buyer's suggested or implied need with, "Here's what we did to help ABC company in a similar situation...." Using real-world illustrations of how your product or service – or your own Counselor skills – helped another client is especially potent because you're tacitly selling yourself through an accomplished deed, not on the prospect of what you might do in the current scenario. For example, a machine parts salesman might use this reference: "A couple of months ago, we got involved in a project with Simmons Machine – I think you might know of them. They were having problems holding some very tight tolerances on some difficult, cylindrical shapes – very small ones. They were ruining three out of every

Pride Goeth Before a Fall

Claire was hired to sell a new computer software application for industrial inventory management. She graduated first in her class in college and had created several profitable inventory management software systems while still in school. Unfortunately, she made it clear to every prospect or client that she felt she was the most knowledgeable person in the field. She assumed she knew all about their problems, without researching their special needs or their organization's cultural and political quirks. Sure, she possessed obvious technical mastery, but her haughtiness and inflexibility led to problems with client retention. Claire's product had no shortage of able competitors, and most of the clients who cut her loose figured they could find another salesperson with a better mix of people and technical skills.

10 parts with conventional machining techniques. We came up with a way to handle that problem that has cut their scrap down to almost zero."

• Using statements like, "What I know about your situation is this…" But beware of making educated guesses when you have little solid (or verifiable) information to go on. You'll lose serious points on competence if you guess wrong about a prospect's needs or the conditions inside his or her company.

It also pays to remember the fine line between competence and arrogance. Competence isn't defined as all-knowing arrogance; trust quickly goes out the window if you debate with customers or try to prove them wrong. Customers often relate to you better when you acknowledge you don't know it all. Respect can grow when you admit that you may not have an answer now, but you'll investigate further and come back quickly with a solution.

Commonality

Plenty of salespeople think commonality means noticing photos of a whitewater-rafting trip on a prospect's wall and then recounting their own dramatic journey down some unruly river with a college room-mate. While the anecdote may be fine if true – and most clients will know when it isn't – establishing commonality requires going a bit deeper with prospects into the area of shared ideals, hopes or even history.

That's not to say you and a prospect must hold the same personal values to establish common ground. You can be at polar opposites on the latest political issue affecting your business, for example, but the fact never has to come up if you're there to sell industrial safety equipment. Sharing *professional* values, however, is a different story. The customer likely will want to know, for instance, that you personally value workplace safety.

Buyers want to know you're the kind of person they can do business with, that they won't have sleepless nights at the thought of working with you, that on a fundamental level you're trustworthy. They want to know that you understand them and what they perceive as their very distinctive needs (which, in reality, are probably quite common). They want to know you're more than a technician; you come with a heart, soul, and sense of humor as well.

Being honest, probing for shared experiences or ideals, and asking open-ended questions ("I've read a lot about that problem lately. What do you think is going to happen next?") will carry you far toward establishing commonality. Minor similarities gradually linked together can form a strong, common base.

But none of these practices are without pitfalls. Plenty of topics and straightforward opinions easily spark disagreement, so you'll want to corral the conversation if it strays too far from business and steer it back to more productive territory.

One of the best ways to build commonality, according to Wilson Learning Worldwide research, is to mention a third party who may have referred you to a potential buyer. That individual's credibility with the buyer tends to be transferred to you, the Counselor salesperson. We call this trust by proxy: The prospect trusts you because a friend he or she trusts says that you're okay.

Intent

We've all been there. It's the last call of the day, and, if we close this sale, we collect the quarterly bonus. No matter how hard we try to camouflage it, customers can sense we care more about making that sale today than we do about helping them think through a complex problem, which might take until tomorrow, next week or next month.

Of the four trust-building dimensions, *intent* carries the most weight in establishing credibility. Intent – one's motive – can be a particular challenge for salespeople, since our mission is to ask for the order and capture the business. There's no massaging it.

Good intent implies a win-win relationship. That means a relationship where the buyer wins by having a problem solved, and the salesperson wins by having solved a problem and made a sale. Your challenge as a salesperson is to communicate the feeling of win-win as quickly as possible to create a good buying climate for the rest of the sales interview and, indeed, for the duration of a long client relationship.

Key to the indication of our intentions is how we plan to work with the buyer. Do we plan to dictate a solution? Do we plan to show only those items that will win us a trip to the Bahamas? Do we plan to make recommendations based on incomplete knowledge of the buyer's unique situation?

If your every "touch point" or contact with customers involves asking for business, it won't take long for them to grow irritated or adopt a resentful, "What has she done for me lately?" attitude. Buyers aren't naïve; they know when you truly care about what they think versus when you're playing a role. Prospects and clients need to perceive that you have their best interests at heart as well as your own.

Intent gets to the heart of the Counselor philosophy. When you're willing to help buyers do more than purchase product, when you work with them to build lasting solutions and acquire new insights into their

Back to the Basics:
Propriety and Commonality in Action

Terror was the operative emotion as Tom Jamieson pondered a major career change to insurance sales. Jamieson had spent the first 20 years of his professional life as a truck driver and didn't have a college degree. But health problems forced a change in his career path, and he embraced the prospect of helping people provide security for their families or possessions, as well as gaining more control over his own work life.

"I think what scared me the most was that I didn't know what my customers expected from me on the little things," Jamieson says. "The company did a great job training me on its products, but initially I didn't know what the customer thought an insurance salesman should look, act, or sound like. I based my judgements on guesses, as much as anything."

After selling a full line of insurance for a year Jamieson did some research. He noted that his biggest success had come in selling homeowner's and automobile insurance to blue-collar workers. "I reasoned that I just wasn't relating well to white-collar people, yet they were the more lucrative clients. I personally liked my original client base, but wanted to expand it."

So Jamieson went to work on the key Counselor Relating principles of propriety and commonality. He spent two weeks' worth of lunches interviewing friends and relatives who worked at white-collar jobs. "I asked all the obvious and embarrassing questions like, 'What color shirt should I wear?' and 'How should I introduce myself when I meet prospects?' After that I started to adjust my behavior and dress appropriately."

Tom started frequenting restaurants favored by white-collar workers as a fly on the wall. He began reading newspapers and magazines he saw them reading.

Progress was slow, but Jamieson says these efforts helped him overcome problems with propriety and commonality, allowing his competence and intent to shine through with his new target market. Before long, he had made serious inroads into the long-sought white-collar arena.

own business or industry, when you provide valuable extra service, they begin to think of you more as an advisor than a product pusher. But intent cannot be presented in words; it must be backed up with behavior. Some behaviors that demonstrate intent include:

- Follow through on commitments. Reliability isn't a "sometimes" thing.
- Tone of voice. It communicates no stress or frustration, regardless of what happens to the hoped-for sale.
- Body language. It is open and professional at all times, never defensive or disappointed.

Objectivity and humility also aid intent. When you acknowledge that your product can't solve every problem in every situation, that it may have weaknesses as well as many strengths, you build credibility. If prospects see that you're willing to admit to your own limitations and humanness, they're a lot more likely to open up themselves.

That level of honesty also serves as a differentiator by virtue of its rarity. The Counselor salesperson sets realistic expectations and then consistently delivers on them, rather than over promising and under delivering.

PROVE YOUR GOOD INTENTIONS WITH THE 3 Ps

When you show you care about helping the customer, not just about boosting your own numbers, you've built the foundation for a long-term relationship through your good intent. Showing propriety, competence, and commonality will get you there even faster.

You can more effectively demonstrate your good intent by regularly using the 3P system in sales interviews: purpose, process, and payoff. By communicating these three things succinctly and accurately in terms of your customer's business, your intent becomes clear. Remember that the greatest cause of "no trust" is the prospect's unfamiliarity or suspicion with our intentions.

It helps to write them down as brief statements:

Purpose   Answer the question, "Why am I here?" Even if the prospect already knows what kind of business you represent and even though you may have discussed it generally by phone or e-mail, it's a good idea to clarify your role as a problem solver by stating the reason for your visit.

For example, "My purpose today is to share some information about myself, my company, and the products and services we offer, and to find out more about your company and your needs. Is this agreeable to you?"

Process   Show the customer the process you intend to use to achieve that stated purpose. This helps reduce tension and uncertainty because the buyer knows exactly what to expect.

You might say, "I'd like to begin by discussing some questions I thought you may have about my company and me and then explore any additional problems or needs you want to talk about."

Payoff   Answer the question, "How will we both benefit from taking this valuable time out of our busy days?" Don't forget to include the payoff for you, or the customer will note your lack of honesty. After all, this is a business relationship.

A sample payoff statement: "You'll learn something about us, we'll learn something about you, and together we'll determine whether I am (or my company is) a potential resource for meeting your needs."

BUILD EMPATHY BY EMULATING BEN DUFFY

Ben Duffy was a sales executive at a large New York advertising agency in the 1960s. When he discovered the American Tobacco Company was looking for a new advertising agency, he used his industry contacts to secure an appointment with an important marketing executive at the company. The day before the meeting, he got a hotel room and began drafting a presentation. Then he tore it up and began again. And again. Frustrated as he saw the sun setting, he was wracking his brain for ways to impress this savvy executive when he came up with an idea: he would pretend he was the executive. If he were running the marketing department at American Tobacco, what questions would he ask of a prospective ad agency?

Ben crafted 10 questions with the accompanying answers. When he met with the executive, he introduced himself and told the executive what he'd done. At this point, the executive interrupted Ben and said, "That's very interesting, Mr. Duffy, because right after your call, I did exactly the same thing. I made up my own list of 10 questions. How'd you like to share lists?"

Well, put yourself in Ben Duffy's shoes. Millions of dollars of business were riding on the simple exchange of a pair of lists. So the two men traded, and gradually both began to smile. Seven of the executive's ten questions matched Ben's.

It's no surprise that Ben's agency landed the account. In fact, that agency and American Tobacco Company worked together for over 20 years. The reason? Ben showed he could empathize with the customer. He could see the world (and himself) from the customer's point of view, understand the customer's unique challenges or concerns, and from that foundation, sculpt a winning sales approach.

Every Counselor salesperson can do the same thing by using some simple steps:

Before the call:

1. Think about the buyer's likely concerns, issues, and questions. Conduct research inside and outside the company to help establish those issues.
2. List the concerns or issues in the form of questions. Remember, you are writing your list as if you were the buyer.
3. Develop responses to those questions.

You'll likely notice many of your questions address the four key dimensions of trust building we've just examined.

When making the call:

1. Share the the two or three very best questions you prepared.
2. Check that the questions are on target. If yes, proceed to step 4.
3. Ask about additional concerns.
4. Answer questions. Include responses to any information you gained from step 3.

The Ben Duffy approach has clear benefits for the beginning stages of any sales relationship, but also has merit for established, ongoing client relationships, where it's easy to let your attention drift into autopilot. To keep abreast of the changing needs or desires of your tenured customers, periodically consider asking (and answering, Ben Duffy style) these questions:

- Why do we remain the best company for you to partner with?
- What results have we produced for your company or business unit?
- What experience do our employees have with your industry?

You may discover some long-time customers are very anxious to learn (and justify to their bosses) why they continue to keep their business with you, especially with emerging or established competitors dangling attractive new offers by the week.

AN ACTION PLAN FOR IMPROVING RELATING SKILLS

As we mentioned at the beginning of the chapter, everyone has the ability to build trust by establishing credibility and showing empathy. The goal is to work consciously on your trust-building skills so you can more quickly reduce relationship tension and transition into productive phases of a business interaction. To that end, try these tactics:

35

- Follow through on every commitment you make to a client or prospect, no matter how small, even at the expense of having to cancel introductory meetings with new prospects.

- Read trade publications and glean 3 pieces of news, research, or insight about the industries you serve. Subtly work that knowledge into your customer meetings.

- Obtain the annual report from a client or prospect's company. Read the summary before you meet with each client.

- Look for small favors you can do for prospects or clients that send a message you're looking out for their best interests, and don't just view them as human cash machines.

- Prepare detailed examples of how the product or service you're selling has helped other clients with similar needs or problems.

- Find the names of industry leaders and call them for 10-minute informational interviews. Mention the fact you talked to those people in meetings with prospects.

- Videotape yourself giving a mock presentation. Note your body language, and work to make it comfortable and open. Consider getting a professional critique of your presentation style.

- Write Purpose/Process/Payoff statements for every customer meeting.

- Use the Ben Duffy approach for all your customers, including long-time customers.

3 | Discovering the Discovery Process

You've laid the foundation for a successful sales relationship. The buyer feels
comfortable with you, has evidence
of your sincerity, competence, and
good intentions, and is beginning
to open up. Still, something isn't
quite right. Although the buyer
may trust that you won't steer him
wrong, a time-honored objection still
rings in your ears: "It seems to be a
quality product with a competitive price,
but we just don't need it."

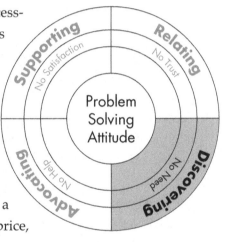

Understanding and working to avoid this barrier of "no need" –
through what we call *Discovery* skills – is perhaps the most critical step
in the Counselor-selling process.

DISCOVERING IN THE COUNSELOR SELLING ERA

Back in the basic needs-based selling era, described in Chapter 1, Discovering was relatively simple. You asked the customers questions to
make sure you understood what they said they needed, you matched
the products or services you offered to those needs and, when there
was a match, you moved on to recommending your solution.

But in the Counselor selling era, a lot has changed. Customers have
a much broader selection of products and services with a wide variety

of customizable features available. Customer problems and needs have also grown more complex, especially in the business-to-business selling environment. The result leads to one critical fact about Discovering in the Counselor selling era:

Customers know what their problems are,
But they don't always know what their needs are.

What customers know best are their problems, goals, and their vision of the future. However, given the range of options for achieving their vision, customers sometimes need help prioritizing the importance of solving each problem, uncovering the root causes of their problems, and identifying the best solutions among many.

So what's a problem? What's a need? Consider this: a friend of ours recently had problems with moles in his garden. The moles dug underground, eating the roots of the plants and grass. On the surface, the problem and need seem simple:

- Problem: moles are killing my garden.
- Need: get rid of the moles.

A needs-based salesperson, having discovered this, might try to sell our friend devices to trap, kill, or drive off the moles. But a Counselor salesperson goes deeper into the problem, using his or her own expertise in the area to work with the customer and discover (here, literally uncover) the root cause and priorities. The result might be something like this:

- Problem: moles are killing my garden.
- Fact: moles are in the garden because I have grubs, and moles eat grubs.
- Fact: The grubs are in the garden because the earth is damp, and grubs love damp soil.

- Fact: the garden is damp because of poor drainage.
- Feeling: my family thinks it is cruel to trap and kill the moles.

Now the Counselor salesperson and the customer both have a better understanding of the problem, related facts and feelings, and a broader range of options for defining the need and solving the problem. The customer also knows now that killing or driving off the moles will only result in a temporary solution (the moles will return if the grubs are still there). He'll solve his mole problems much more effectively by killing the grubs, or even better, improving the drainage.

TWEAKING THE GOLDEN RULE

The upshot is you can't sell effectively in the face of "no need," and you can't be a real problem solver until you and the customer share an understanding of the problem. In Counselor selling, Discovery becomes a mutual process, with you and the customer working hand-in-hand. The customer's knowledge of his or her problems and situation mix with the Counselor's expert knowledge of products, services, or capabilities.

Counselors use expert questioning, listening, and restatement skills to get at the root causes of the customer's problems, to help the customer prioritize his or her needs and motives, and to uncover related, but hidden problems that affect the success of the solution. Discovery operates on the still-novel notion that buyers, not salespeople, define what's valuable or unique about a product or service placed before them. So until that critical intelligence is gathered and synthesized, any sales presentation is premature.

The Golden Rule tells us we should "do unto others as you would have them do unto you." At the risk of heresy, the Counselor Approach doesn't fully subscribe to that theory. Rather, it suggests, *"do unto others the way they want and need to have done unto them."*

As a pillar of Counselor selling, Discovery suggests that trying to fit a prospect to a presentation, rather than vice versa, is a sure path to long-term failure. When the salesperson starts out by pushing the incomparable or market-leading features of his product, the customer may see, absent good Discovery, the product as a square peg for a round hole. The salesperson may point to exhaustive market research or past sales success as "proof" that the world needs his product. But what about the prospect standing in front of him right now? Are her needs the same as the last customer who bought the product? Is she even clear on her own needs? The Counselor uses Discovery to sell within the context of each customer's specific situation and buying motives.

"Discovery is the most important part of the sales process by far," says Jan Broll, a Wilson Learning Worldwide account executive. "Your solution can only be as good as the information you have about the buyer. As a result, your ability to differentiate your product or service relies on your ability to find information your competitor doesn't have."

Salespeople without good Discovery skills often find, usually too late, that they've been shadow boxing rather than truly engaging buyers. Or they find that they've tried to force-feed solutions to prospects in a marketplace where the competition will custom fit their solutions to meet the prospect's unique needs.

Indeed, selling isn't getting any easier. The traditional persuader or features expert has a much tougher go of it in today's global business climate. Global competition ensures customers will continue to have more choices than ever before. They perceive less differentiation between products, and often experience more price flattening. The Internet closes off another advantage. These days, surfing customers often have as much information about both your own and the competing products as you do, and they are increasingly sophisticated about buying products and services.

The bottom line: either you flex to meet customers' needs, or watch today's increasingly challenging customer find a better fit with another seller.

Stormy Weather: How Poor Discovery Botched One Sale

After several years of changing heavy external storm windows every spring and fall, I decided to get vinyl combination windows to match those in my sunporch. They switch from glass window to screen by simply sliding the right pane up or down.

We invited a sales representative from the window company that made the sunporch windows to our home one evening. We wanted to buy as many windows of the same model as we could afford. If we couldn't buy them all at once, we would buy some now and some later.

The young man who showed up was well dressed and very polite. After a few minutes of chatting, he set up an easel. I asked him if he didn't want to talk with us first about what we were interested in. He said no, because he was going to tell us about the best windows available anyway, and we could choose among them after he was finished. I preferred not to do it that way. I wanted him to look at the vinyl windows we had so he could tell us about windows that were similar. He reluctantly agreed to look at the windows.

Then he began his presentation – from the top. I tolerated it for a few minutes, thinking that we could simply pick out the closest match from those he showed us. But the presentation soon went to a specific model that must have been on the sales manager's "push" list for the month. When I mentioned that this model was different from the ones we liked, he said that this was a superior model, and urged us to order it now for the rest of the house – and then eventually upgrade the windows on the porch to match!

We thanked him for his interesting presentation and said that we would think about it. The next day we went shopping at the retail outlets of other companies and bought a dozen windows that were the closest match to what we had. We put them on the second floor and the first floor front. The next year we went back to the same outlet and ordered the same model number for the rest of the house.

What does this story show? No need and no help. The salesperson made no effort to discover our unique needs and made a presentation that was no help to us.

– Tom Kramlinger

SHINING A LIGHT ON UNSEEN NEEDS

Discovery provides competitive advantage because it gives salespeople the ability to dig quickly and tactfully beneath a prospect's initial, surface problem to expose hidden problems and needs that the customer might not even be aware of. In reality, these needs or problems have always been there, but the prospect may not see them without the help and guidance of the Counselor. In other cases, status quo thinking is the culprit: What's "not broken" does, in fact, often need to be fixed. Once the salesperson helps the prospect prioritize the problems, see the root causes, and identify linked problems, the need to do something rapidly follows.

Witness Isotech, a Baltimore-based company that developed automation software for hospital record keeping. Physicians had been keeping patients' records in physical files for decades. Sure, a few got misplaced or lost now and again, but those instances were so rare there was little reason to think about changing or upgrading the system. The famed Mayo Clinic in Rochester, Minnesota claimed to have lost only one patient file in all its years of operation, with hundreds of thousands of patients served.

So how does a salesperson convince a group of inherently conservative professionals to fix something that doesn't appear to be broken? "We worked with one small medical clinic to determine the cost of everything from staffing the records department, to losing a file, to a physician making a bad decision because a file wasn't updated quickly enough," says sales rep Beth Montgomery, who worked for the fledgling firm at the time of the product launch at the dawn of the computerized record keeping era. "We talked to everyone, including the file clerks, nurses and doctors, the patients, janitors, and pharmacists, to make sure we covered every aspect of the situation."

Isotech used a Discovery process to identify problems that neither it nor the prospective client was even sure existed, eventually showing the clinic that investing in its record-keeping software would improve patient care and reduce the clinic's costs.

This is different from prompting customers to tell you what they already know. That practice isn't true Counselor selling. Many organizations claim their salespeople are "consultative" or practice "consultative selling skills." But what passes for consulting skills is, in most cases, simply the old needs-based selling approach. Discovery adds another dimension to that approach. Counselor selling isn't simply asking questions to determine a customer's needs, listening well to answers, or recommending products that best meet stated needs. It's a process that creates a partnership with the customer to explore the problems deeply enough to understand clearly the true needs and opportunities. At this point, and *only* at this point, does the customer realize he or she needs to make a buying decision.

> ## Catching the Client's Feelings and Attitudes
>
> Bill Gove, an accomplished salesperson, once said, "Effective therapists are often called good 'catchers' because they are able to catch the client's feelings and attitudes. Maybe salespeople would be more effective if they became less concerned with the sales pitch, or sales message, and more concerned with the sales catch. Sure, professional salespeople give the prospect reasons why it's better to buy now than delay...but if they're wise, they make sure the reasons they give are the prospect's reasons and not theirs."

DIGGING INTO THE GAP: THE DISCOVERY AGREEMENT

One of the most effective ways to guide buyers to identify unsolved problems or unfulfilled needs – needs they may not be fully aware of – is to conduct a formal assessment of the Gap between their "Haves" and "Wants." Under "Haves," you include the buyer's current situation, his history and background, business unit or organizational problems and root causes, and the consequences of those problems. Under "Wants," include the buyer's desired situation: hoped-for changes, improvements or competitive advantage to be gained from a purchase; personal and task related motives involved in a buying decision; and more. The Counselor's role is not to tell the customer what he already knows – that his haves and wants are different – rather, the Counselor concentrates on addressing the Gap.

The power of discovery lies in its ability to define and work with the Gap. You may be very clear about both what the buyer has and wants, but unclear about the Gap, or the buyer's problem. Good discovery directly asks the buyer, "Why *don't* you have what you want?" or "What's *keeping* you from getting what you want?" Asking this final set of questions, directly, elicits the real problem from the buyer and clarifies what it will take to close the Gap. Many salespeople think all they have to do is find out what the client has and wants, and then give them what they want. They are shocked later to hear, "There's no budget for this," or "The CFO won't approve this," or "The culture won't endorse this." If you really understand what keeps the Gap *open*, you will reveal what it takes to *close* it.

The culmination of identifying Gaps between "Haves" and "Wants" is a written or verbal *Discovery Agreement* (see the Model Discovery Agreement on page 46). This is a pivotal part of Counselor selling. The Discovery Agreement summarizes what the buyer has and what the buyer wants, and confirms that you, as salesperson, have a firm grasp of the buyer's needs. Your buyer's confirmation and acceptance gives you a green light to begin developing a solution for your customer – to begin narrowing the Gap.

A Discovery Agreement is **not** a contract or proposal. It summarizes the salesperson's (and hopefully the customer's) understanding of the problems and needs. Discovery Agreements do not name, or even hint at, a specific approach to solving the problem. One of the biggest mistakes salespeople make is trying to present the statement of the problem and the proposed solution together. This does not give the customer a chance to agree with the problem statement and makes the solution look like just another canned recommendation.

The Gap – What Keeps Buyers from Getting What They Want

The **Gap** springs from the buyer's environment: budget, priorities, politics, culture, readiness, market conditions, etc.

HAVE	GAP	WANT
History, background	**G**	Changes, improvements
Problems, causes	**A**	Advantages, gains
Impact, consequences	**P**	Higher level of satisfaction
Level of satisfaction		Personal motives
Buying roles, conditions		Task motives

The **Discovery Agreement** summarizes what the buyer has and what the buyer wants, and confirms that you understand the buyer's problem – the Gap.

If your prospect doesn't immediately agree with your summary, don't be disappointed. Instead, be thankful you didn't move on to your solutions presentation based on an inaccurate or incomplete understanding of the prospect's problem. Non-agreement is thus almost as valuable as agreement. As you and the customer correct and refine the Discovery Agreement, the customer becomes increasingly committed to the description of the problem and the importance of solving it. In the end, what you want is a Discovery Agreement that the customer feels like he or she wrote.

DISCOVERY'S VITAL ENGINE: THE ART OF QUESTIONING

Creating a Discovery Agreement requires a great deal of input from the customer and polished interviewing skills on the part of the salesperson. It takes certain skills to be a successful interviewer, skills few of us

Written Discovery Agreement – Nick Helms

Dear Mr. Taylor,

I would like to thank you for the time and information you shared with me at our recent meeting. I would like to clarify our discussion to this point, in order to make sure that I am on the right track in understanding your situation.

Current status:

- The company has grown fast and you have your hands full simply keeping everything going. Thus, you have not had much time to think about the staff's needs for snacks and drinks.
- Right now there are no formal canteen facilities. For snacks, employees go across the road to a snack shop; for drinks, the separate offices make their own arrangements.
- There is no consistency in these arrangements and there are cases where they don't always work smoothly, as evidenced by bickering in the offices about whose turn it is to make drinks.
- You are concerned about the time people spend walking across the road to the snack shop during the work day.

Desired status:

- Your key concern is to have the team operating smoothly, particularly when there is a launch on. In response to this concern:
  1. You are interested in ways to save staff time and improve efficiency.
  2. You would like the staff to feel that the company is looking after them and is involved in caring about them.

I hope I have captured the salient points of our discussion. Please make any additions or corrections.

Recommended next step:

Based upon what you have told me, I would like to meet with Mary to find out what she and the rest of the staff might need from a new service. After my meeting with Mary, you and I would then meet to discuss the options.

I believe that our company can help you keep your staff going with hot and cold drinks, and snacks, not only during normal times, but also through those periods of high activity. I will call you Tuesday afternoon to review this understanding with you and set a day and time for our meeting.

Sincerely,

Nick Helms
Account Manager

are born with. Most good interviewers have consciously learned and refined their art.

To create a quality Discovery Agreement, you'll need to expand your efforts to uncover buying needs or preferences beyond an organization's identified "decision makers." You'll also need to interview others who influence purchase decisions, whether subtly or overtly (for more on dealing with these "purchase influencers," see pages 52-54). Such well-rounded Discovery and research lessens the odds of being ambushed by hidden influencers.

Given the varied backgrounds and motives of buyers and purchase influencers, developing various types of Discovery questions to ask them will help you unearth valuable information and ensure you've covered all your bases.

Some useful question types include:

Permission: The permission question signals the go-ahead to begin Discovery. Simply ask, "Would you mind if I ask a few questions about your business?" If the answer is, "Go right ahead," you've entered the Discovery zone.

Fact-Finding: These questions answer the fundamentals of who, what, when, where, and how much. As such, they give you a complete picture of the customer's current operation, laying the groundwork for your future sales strategy. Because fact-finding questions generally produce little tension, many salespeople prefer them as a good way to open an interview.

Let's say you sell skid loaders for use on construction projects. Your fact-finding questions might include:

- How many different construction projects do you typically have going at once? How many days do you typically need skid loaders at each project?

47

- Do you usually rent or buy skid loaders?
- Do you use full-time employees or contract workers to run the skid loaders? When do you tend to employ each type of worker?
- Do you have in-house maintenance for the loaders or do you contract that work out?

Notice that while most of these questions pertain to the "Have" side of the gap, you'll begin to get a glimpse of the "Want" side as you start comparing data collected to industry averages or historical performance at the company.

Feeling-Finding: While fact-finding questions usually elicit short answers containing verifiable, objective data, feeling-finding questions ask what the customer feels and thinks about known facts, and aim to determine needs, wants or expectations.

Combined with their fact-finding counterparts, these questions can be a powerful way to lead customers to important "ahas!" or realizations about current problems or opportunities. For example, while posing fact-finding questions, our skid loader salesperson might also ask:

- How do you feel about the overall quality of your current equipment?
- What would it mean to you to cut your repair costs in half?
- What do you think about your current maintenance program?

Notice the use of the words *think* and *feel*. These help unearth buyers' opinions, values, feelings and beliefs.

Best/Least: Another method for discovering more about the "Have" side of the gap is to ask customers what they like best and least about their current situations. Testing the extremes is an effective means of intensifying the difference between what prospects have and what they want. It's particularly helpful in situations where you're selling

Paired Fact-Finding and Feeling-Finding Questions

Fact-Finding Questions	Feeling-Finding Questions
What kind of equipment are you using now?	What kind of equipment would you like to have?
How many units does it produce per day?	How many units do you feel you should produce per day?
When does it require maintenance?	What do you think is a better maintenance schedule?
Who is needed to operate it?	What is your biggest worry in terms of manpower?
Does it ever break down?	What is the main reason for the downtime?
How much do these repairs cost?	What would it mean to you to cut your repair costs in half?
How much downtime have you had?	What do you think should be done to reduce that downtime?
Are you going to meet your contract deadline?	How important is it to meet your contract deadline?
Who's in charge of the project?	Who would you like to have in charge?
How much control do you have now?	How much control would you like to have?
How visible is the system?	How important is great visibility?
Is anyone else doing it now?	What do you think about being first?
What are the others saying about it?	How much would you like their agreement?
Who do they blame when it happens?	Who do you wish they would blame?
Did you design this yourself?	How much of your own input should be in the new design?
What kind of feedback are you getting?	To what degree must the feedback be perfect?

against a competitive product that the prospect is already using. If you have a feeling the prospect is sticking with the status quo when he shouldn't be, testing the extremes is a good way to guide him to a realization that the present situation is unsatisfactory.

It usually works best to pose the positive question first – what does the customer like best? – since the answer describes the performance you must match or exceed in your proposed solution.

Our skid loader salesperson, for instance, might ask: "What do you like best about your current fleet of skid loaders?" followed by, "What is the one thing you would change about the fleet?"

Magic Wand: Everyone deserves a chance to dream – if only for the moment – and dreams often fuel the "Want" side of the gap. Ask prospects what changes or improvements they would make if budgets, time, organizational politics, or other limitations didn't stand in their way. With today's fast-evolving technology, you may already have a solution to help achieve one or more of those dreams.

Catch -All: These questions invite the customer to complete the picture and frequently elicit concerns or issues you may not have thought of. A typical catch-all, posed at the end of an interview, might be "Is there anything else it would be helpful to know about your operation? Something I should have asked and didn't?"

TWO EARS, ONE MOUTH: THE VALUE OF LISTENING WELL

Good Discovery relies on good questioning technique, yet all the questioning skill in the world won't mean much if you're not skilled at absorbing, clarifying, and expanding on what prospects tell you. Good listening skills are essential to building credible Discovery Agreements. And if you develop your skills to a high level, you may find answers to questions you didn't think to ask.

Rather than talking prospects into buying, the Counselor more frequently *listens* them into buying. As we said earlier, people do not like to be sold, yet they love to buy. In a prospect's mind, "talking" by the salesperson equates to being sold. "Listening" by the salesperson means buying.

According to Wilson Learning Worldwide research, listening acumen ranks second only to product knowledge as a critical competency for salespeople. Yet listening is also among the most difficult skills to master, due in part to cultural norms, education shortfalls, and our own busy lives. The business world expects and teaches us to multi-task. As a result, when we should be fully engaged in dialogue with a buyer, we think instead of our next question, our next sales call, or our next meeting with our manager. Most of us let our minds drift the second a buyer struggles to define his needs, challenges, or feelings.

Committing full energy to the moment is hard work, but you can overcome bad habits and become a responsive listener by consciously changing your listening style. A good listener is like a submarine radar technician, listening for the "pings" and zeroing in on the customers needs, moving closer and closer to the targeted area of interest with every statement.

Some listening techniques to practice:

- Restate or paraphrase a prospect's key thoughts or comments. Think of beginnings like "So what you are saying is…" or "In other words…" or "Let me see if I understand…". Caution: Use this technique sparingly, or it will appear forced. Reserve it for summarizing at the end of a major topic area or the conclusion of the entire discussion.
- Ask questions that clarify a buyer's comments. These "checking" questions often follow a restatement and are used to make sure you understand information just delivered. Think of questions such as, "Did you say you are laying off 20 percent of your production workers?" "So productivity is a primary objective, is that correct?" or "Is it fair to assume that…?"

- Whenever you ask a question, especially a feeling-finding question, allow prospects enough time to start talking. If they pause, encourage them to continue, resisting the temptation to interrupt or embellish what was said. Remaining an attentive listener can win you more sales than any persuasive picture you might be tempted to paint.
- Use a listening posture – good eye contact, unfolded arms, a slight lean toward the speaker, and frequent head nods.
- Minimize your note taking to ensure active engagement in the conversation.

If we were to conduct a survey among all the salespeople in the world about to make a sales call right now, chances are we'd discover that 50 percent have absolutely no idea what questions they're going to ask a prospect, 40 percent have a general idea, and only 10 percent have a good idea. Of that 10 percent, probably only one in 10 has a written list.

How about you? To which of those groups do you belong? Why not put together your own checklist of fact-finding and feeling-finding questions? Take it with you on each call and adapt or add to it for each prospect. You only have to write out your master list once. From then on, it'll pay dividends in every interview.

DON'T OVERLOOK PURCHASE INFLUENCERS IN DISCOVERY

As you pursue fact-finding to determine prospects' Have/Want gaps, you'll probably notice a common phenomenon: More people in the organization begin weighing in on the buying decision. In some scenarios, you'll deal only with one decision maker, but in more complex or big-ticket sales transactions, there will be many *purchase influencers*. You'll need to factor them into your Discovery efforts.

Some of these influencers are peripheral players who'll offer their input and then fade away. Others will play a larger, ongoing role in determining whether you land the business. And, like a theater troupe, these players can change roles depending on the nature and staging of a purchase.

It's your job to identify these purchase influencers and what roles they play, because you'll most likely need to spend some Discovery time with all of them. This means gaining their trust and learning their unique perspectives on the company's needs.

To that end, you'll want to add a few questions to your repertoire to clarify the roles this ensemble group will play in awarding new business. Some questions to ask are:

- What is your role in selecting new products or services?
- Who else is involved in the decision? Where does he or she fit in the organization?
- How many of those people will need to sign off on any proposed solution?
- Who supervises use of the product or service?
- Are there any outside consultants who'll be involved?
- Is there anyone else I should talk to in order to get a full picture of the company's needs?

Many salespeople find it indispensable to obtain (or create on their own) an organizational chart of the prospect company to determine who reports to whom and who is responsible for what. That kind of information can be obtained through many sources: clients, client-employees, or third parties familiar with the organization, for example.

It's not only important to know who may influence a decision, but also to know how and to what degree – in other words, to have some grasp of company politics. In that sense, it can be useful to ask a company source with whom you've developed a level of trust:

- Who listens to whom?
- Which people will likely have the most impact on this decision?
- How do they get along?

Be especially wary of *hidden influencers*. For example, when companies first began installing new Internet technologies, many top managers turned to their college age – or even teenage – sons and daughters when they were searching for buying advice. In the case of our skid loader salesperson, he may find he also has to sell some of the organization's front-line workers on his product because they strongly influence the foreman who sits on the purchasing committee. These workers are, after all, the ones who use the machines every day.

While hidden influencers might seem difficult to identify, there are ways to find them and win their support before they mount quiet opposition to your selling efforts. A few ideas:

- Listen closely for cues:
    - Does your contact frequently mention other influential people in a casual way during your business discussions?
    - Do you frequently see the same co-worker/friend in the client's office when you arrive for a meeting?
    - Is there a sudden change in direction in terms of the depth or breadth of the information the client asks for?

If you suspect a hidden influencer, be straightforward and ask if the client has some new advisors. Don't act surprised. Mention that it's perfectly natural to seek advice from the outside, and then find out as much as you can about this new player. If appropriate, ask if you can meet the person or send materials to him or her.

No matter how misguided the hidden influencer's advice seems to be, don't criticize the person. He or she could be a dear friend or even the prospect's child. Any show of frustration or lack of respect will quickly degrade the trust you've worked so hard to build.

AVOID THESE DISCOVERY FAUX PAS

Discovery Agreements are powerful documents, and like anything with power they can be used for positive or harmful purposes. Here

Avoiding the Presentation Temptation

We all know that asking good questions is the best way to discover customers' unique problems or challenges. But what if a busy prospect resists such inquiry, eager to get to the pitch? What if he or she just wants you to get on with your presentation, effectively shutting the door to Discovery efforts? That's a problem, but it's not insurmountable.

When a prospect puts cart before horse by asking, "How much does that thing cost?" or "Tell me specifically how the product works," you'll be tempted to dive into your product story. Don't do it.

If you start to present now, you're giving yourself top billing at precisely the wrong moment. At this stage of the process, the prospect ought to have the starring role. You can't discover anything while you're talking. But you can discover an awful lot by listening.

"If I don't take time first to learn what's important to the buyer, then my story does no good," says Sara Wuest, an account representative for Silicon Graphics Inc., the Mountain View, California manufacturer of supercomputers. "I'm not going to sell something if the prospect doesn't have a need, and I'm not going to understand that need if I don't understand the prospect as a person."

Develop some phrases to help you reset the interviewing agenda when a prospect pushes prematurely for a presentation. Here are a few starters:

- "Believe me, I'm anxious to tell you about my product, because I think it just might help solve your problem. But before we get into that, let me ask you, what's been the average life span of your undercarriages (or whatever the product/service you're selling) up until now?"

- "You know, Mr. Jensen, the effectiveness of our system depends a lot on the way you plan to use it and the options you might want. So maybe before I get started, you could just give me a brief background on how you're doing it now."

are three temptations to avoid when working with a client's Discovery Agreement:

- **"I know something you don't know."** A Discovery Agreement shouldn't be used to gain access to other decision-makers in the company. Many a naïve (or desperate) sales rep has used a Discovery document to gain the ear of top management with the promise of "exposing" problems in the company. Such moves usually backfire, crushing any trust created with primary lower-level contacts and sometimes turning the sales rep and his or her company into pariahs.

- **"There are a lot of problems here."** No manager likes to hear the area he or she oversees is rife with problems, no matter how apparent those problems may be. It can be tempting to slant a Discovery Agreement toward a company's shortcomings – after all, the greater the problems, the greater the odds of establishing a rationale for your solution. Yet it's important to present a balanced and positive picture, or otherwise you may never get past a decision-maker's defensiveness. It can help to slip in reassuring thoughts such as "I saw that same problem in another company" or highlight areas of strength with comments like, "You're an acknowledged industry leader in this area."

- **"Hey everybody, this is interesting."** The Discovery document contains a great deal of sensitive information – although it may not seem so to you since you've worked so closely with it. It's important not to be cavalier about that sensitivity, nor to grow numb to it. Discovery information shouldn't be shared with sales colleagues outside of your organization, for instance, no matter how much you trust them.

WHY THEY BUY:
IDENTIFYING TASK AND PERSONAL MOTIVES

Every prospect has some overriding motive for making a purchase. We tend to think most business decisions are driven by logical or practical motives, more the result of hard data than personal emotions. If you've spent more than a few hours as a professional salesperson, however, you know that's not always the case. Every purchase, from a pair of blue jeans to a multimillion-dollar telecommunications system, taps deeper into a buyer's psyche on some level.

Purchase motivation can be tough to pin down. Ask four people who purchased the same product why they bought, and you'll probably get four different answers. But identifying what motivates your customer is critical to selecting and shaping the right sales strategy. Some proven tactics can help you do it.

First, let's look at those rational motives. We call them *task motives,* and they typically involve financial or productivity issues. As you move along in the Discovery process, you'll hear buyers talk openly about four such motives: the need to increase profits, decrease costs, boost production and/or quality, or save time and effort. The Counselor's challenge is to discover which of the four task needs is most important to the prospect. At times, of course, buyers have multiple motives or feel some combination of task needs simultaneously. But usually one of the four turns out to be the dominant issue.

Personal motives can be harder to divine since they come from deeper down in the psyche. Because they are personal and often relate to ego, most people try to hide them, rarely, if ever, mentioning them directly. This creates the illusion that task motives are all that matter. Yet we know that people tend to buy as much from the heart as the head. So it's important to try to identify those emotional reasons for purchases, even though you may not feel equipped to deal with something as changeable and ambiguous as personal motives. But by acquiring a basic understanding of them, you can delve beneath the superficial and do a better job helping prospects discover, understand, and act on motivational forces that are most important to them.

In general, look for four types of personal buying motives:

Buying Motives and Personal Appeals

Task Motives and Appeals

Task motives can be defined as logical, practical, and functional reasons for buying.

• More output or quality Is it worth the price? Is it the best?	• Less cost Will it save money? Will it save time?
• Less effort How well will it work for us?	• More profit Will it make money?

Personal Motives and Appeals

Personal motives are the individual, personal preferences that spur a person to buy.

• Respect Expertise Research Update	• Power Control Decisions Options
• Approval Popularity Low risk No conflict	• Recognition Visibility Uniqueness Leadership

- **Respect.** A driving motivation for these buyers, who in many cases are technical workers, is to come across as "the expert" and appear as though they made wise decisions. They will be highly interested in independent research, comparison/contrast data and technical information about a product or service. A respect-driven engineer, for example, may decide to buy some new equipment for a lab because research by other professionals in her field indicates that it operates on superior technology.

- **Approval.** Many decision makers feel a strong need to please others through what they buy – regardless of whether the product beats the competition's offerings or is the best fit for organizational needs. They don't want their purchases to upset the status quo or generate controversy. These prospects are looking to reduce risk and avoid internal conflict, and they frequently ask to include more and more people in meetings with you as buying decisions get closer to being made.

- **Power.** This motive is all about control. These prospects are interested in ideas that increase their freedom of action and add to their responsibility. They respond to approaches or features that promise quicker decision making or an ability to achieve results in a more efficient way. For instance, a power-driven purchasing agent who feels that various departments of the company have conflicting inventory or purchasing policies is likely to be open to products, systems, or ideas that consolidate those policies under his single control. You may hear a lot about the "big picture" from him.

- **Recognition.** These buyers want a purchase to result in a major leap for the company – or their own business unit – so that they receive personal kudos. They see the purchase as a step toward increased visibility and as their chance to stand out from the crowd. These buyers are likely to be risk takers, willing to be first to try something innovative. They're prone to talk about awards they've won, speeches given, or notable personalities they've met, and they often hang personal awards or citations in their offices.

Which Is the Real Motive?

It's one thing to create a laundry list of your prospect's possible buying motives, quite another to determine which of those motives is actually driving buying behavior. The following story illustrates the importance of becoming skilled at the latter:

The president of a small, but very creative advertising agency was competing for a new account. The prospect was a large automobile dealer. The president studied the prospect's company carefully, and he and his staff came up with a unique campaign that capitalized on the dealer's reputation for high volume sales.

He was surprised and disappointed when his agency didn't get the business. But he was furious when the dealer's new ad campaign debuted, and he saw the approach of the competitor who had won the account. Every television commercial, every newspaper ad and every radio spot featured Mr. Dealer. "I knew the man had a big ego," said the ad agency president, "but I didn't think he'd throw away money just to satisfy it."

But the fact was that the competing agency had done a better job of discerning the auto dealer's real objective: personal recognition. Certainly more sales and profit were important, but the dealer was looking ahead. He was planning to run for public office a year down the road, and he wanted his name and face in front of the public.

AND NOW, FOR THE WEATHER REPORT...

Every sales situation has unique circumstances that can affect the sale. Some of these are predictable conditions that can be easily planned for and addressed. Others are as capricious as the weather.

Internal influences usually are predictable and controllable. These include an organization's internal processes and protocols for making buying decisions, or certain product specifications that must be met – price, features, delivery conditions, and more. Some organizations have policies and standards concerning return on investment. They expect that every investment or purchase will return a predetermined yield.

A few well-placed questions can help you get a handle on these internal conditions:

- What are your internal procedures for purchases of this level?
- Does your organization have any current standards for this product? Are there any national, regional, or local codes, regulations, or practices governing your relations with vendors?
- Are any studies necessary prior to this kind of decision? Is this a bidding situation?
- Who has ultimate approval after all divisions come to an agreement?

External influences are far less controllable and include factors like the state of the economy, mergers or trends in the industry, union contracts, consumer-group pressures, and more. Yet ignorance of external factors can derail your sales efforts before they leave the station. You need to be aware of any trends or developments in the company, industry, or economy that could cause problems.

Stay on top of external influences by:

- Reading business magazines, trade journals, and the like.
- Reading the prospect or client company's annual and quarterly reports.
- Checking in periodically with industry leaders.
- Staying plugged into the grapevine by talking to friends in the industry or the prospect company.

By using this information you not only save yourself headaches, you can gain additional credibility. The customer will know you've done your homework when you ask:

- How might your proposed merger with ABC corporation affect the approval of this order?

- How has your company responded to the industry's move to digital technology?
- I understand there's a severe labor shortage in your industry. How has that affected your front-line productivity or customer service performance?

4 | Advocating, Presenting and Closing

SECTION 1: THE BASICS OF ADVOCATING

The photocopier. Post-It® notes. Desktop computers. Air travel. What do these products – and countless others like them – have in common? Certainly not immediate acceptance by a skeptical business or consumer market. Most of these innovations were considered impractical or just plain heretical when they were under development; few were thought to have a chance of succeeding on the level of their predecessor products or services. What is the common denominator shared by these revolutionary products and services? Powerful *advocates*, champions and supporters who had the ability to get buyers to see them as fresh solutions to real or even hidden problems, rather than as innovations for innovation's sake.

New products, especially those which challenge the status quo, almost always are greeted initially with skepticism and resistance. Who would think that a "glue that doesn't stick very well" would ultimately become the basis for Post-It® notes? It was because the inventors, Spenser Silver and Art Fry at 3M Corporation, were passionate champions. They made pads of these notes and then passed them out to people. They made them yellow, rather than white, so people would see them and ask about them. Every new idea or approach needs a passionate advocate. The question is: who is the best advocate for your potential sale?

Obviously, salespeople need to truly believe in their own products and services, but being your own advocate will not be enough to make the sale. For the Counselor salesperson, Advocating is not just about being an advocate, but also about making your customer into an advocate for the solution. This will happen naturally if your customer trusts you (thanks to your Relating) and you clearly understand his or her needs (through Discovery). Indeed, while good Relating and Discovering skills are critical to putting you in a position to make a sale, Advocating skills are essential to finishing the job. Regardless of how comfortable prospects feel with you or how sure you are that you understand their unique buying needs, you won't make a sale if *they* don't see how your product or service will help them. That's why the client feeling "no help" is the third major obstacle to anticipate, prevent or deal effectively with in the Counselor-selling process.

Advocating skills are more important in today's global selling environment than ever before. Potential buyers are bombarded with product information; they understand better than ever that your product or service isn't the only game in town. Their complex technical or business problems usually have many different solutions, available through many different sellers. There are also usually multiple buyers or influencers involved in the decision. Some of those influencers may suspect that there's a solution that's cheaper, better, faster, or more complete than yours. Consequently, it's the Counselor salesperson's job to make it undeniably clear that his or her offering provides all the advantages a client needs.

However, it isn't part of the job to turn every "no" into a "yes." The goal of Counselor Advocating isn't to turn every poor or even borderline fit for your product into a paying customer or to persuade customers to buy, regardless of best interests. The purpose of Advocating is to make sure that when your product or service *is* a compelling match – when it clearly meets a real need – prospects never slip away to the competition.

Balancing the Bicycle

We use a bicycle analogy to help understand the role and importance of Advocating skills. Think of the back wheel of this bike as your knowledge, experience, and competence – the technical skills and product knowledge critical to powering your sales efforts. The front wheel, on the other hand, is your people or "soft" skills, the interpersonal, social, or emotional abilities that help steer the bike. Without good front-wheel skills, all the knowledge, technical expertise, or comparative data in the world can't take you where you need to go.

The key is to find the kind of balance between these technical and people skills that produces maximum sales effectiveness. When your front wheel is too large and the back wheel too small – when there's an

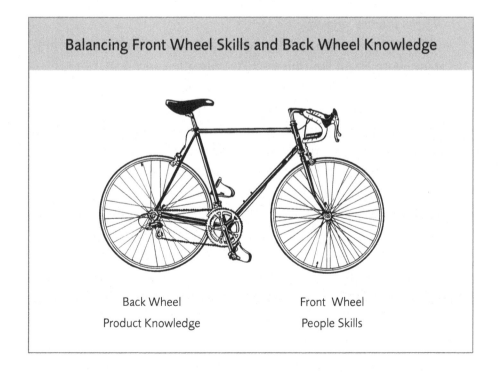

Balancing Front Wheel Skills and Back Wheel Knowledge

Back Wheel
Product Knowledge

Front Wheel
People Skills

abundance of people skills and dearth of technical skills – the bike moves slowly and little gets accomplished. Conversely, if the front wheel is too small and the back wheel too large, you might hit great speeds, but it'll be difficult to steer or control direction, and you'll probably crash along the way.

New salespeople typically have large, powerful back wheels to their bicycles. The majority of their apprenticeships are spent in product knowledge training, learning the ins and outs of product or service features, and understanding how they compare to the competition. If they sell a product line they truly love, or one that's complex, frequently upgraded or amended, they often spend every spare minute learning even more about that product.

Yet it's important to keep these critical back-wheel skills in perspective, to step back and ask a few questions like these, for instance: *Just how much does a prospect truly need to know about all of these features? How would they rank their importance in terms of solving a stated need? When do I need to answer these technical questions myself, and when can I call upon internal support?*

It's impressive when you can answer even the most arcane technical questions about your product. Yet you often only need 20 to 30 percent of that information to close a sale. Remember, customers approach the situation with tunnel vision. They care only about how your offering will solve some particular problem or need of theirs, not how much your firm spent on R&D or design to equip a product with nice-to-have extras the competition doesn't possess.

Listen to the words of Pat Carey, one of IBM's top sales representatives who sells some US$50 million of company product every year: "Anything I sell to my customers they can usually get cheaper somewhere else," Carey says. "For that reason I don't spend time learning every last feature of IBM products. I can find plenty of people in our company who know our products' technical features when I need to know them. *But I can't find anyone who knows my customers' problems like I do.*"

Keith Sondrall, a facilitator who's taught Wilson Learning Worldwide's Counselor-selling process for many years, looks at the front-wheel/back-wheel analogy from an economic standpoint. "In today's global market there are only four ways to differentiate yourself from the competition," Sondrall says. "The first is product superiority. It's great but almost impossible to maintain for long. The second is economic superiority. Your company can sell the same product cheaper than the competition because of economies of scale. That advantage can also be short lived. The third is market identity, which used to mean something. People were 'Honda' families or 'Apple Computer' companies. But with the saturation of quality products and services, customers now know a name isn't everything. That leaves sales acumen and customer service superiority as the only factors we can control."

Avoiding Irrelevance

Without a clear focus on problem-solving purpose, it's easy for your selling efforts to come across as irrelevant, as "nice-to-haves" in what's increasingly a must-have world. The problem of selling features instead of solutions is age-old and particularly acute these days in industries where technical innovation is the norm. Yet it's easy to fall into that trap even in the most ordinary of sales scenarios. For example, even though you may not have military experience, you can probably identify with the soldiers who heard this presentation from their sergeant:

> "All right, you men and women. Today is the day we introduce the new Regulation Missile Whistle, Model M-1. This is a self-repeating, lung-operated, air-cooled-type general personnel model issued to all relevant ranks (he blows the whistle). The whistle is divided into two component parts. These are the Whistle Cylinder Blowing Assembly and the Whistle Retaining Chain Assembly Mechanism. At the Blowing Aperture, there

are two raised sections. You people in the back had better stand up so you can see this. The opening from the blowing end into the main cylinder is called the Compression Blow Channel. The remaining component part of the whistle is known as the Chamber Binder Operating Assembly Complex. This consists of the Opening Sound Admission Slot, the Cylinder Butt Lock onto which the Whistle Retaining Chain Assembly Part is attached, and the Cylinder Reverberating Operating Cork Pellet Device."

Well, that's one way to make a presentation. And it is fairly impressive. But we think the sergeant would have been more effective if he had remembered that people don't buy our products and services. They buy only what they imagine our products or services will do for them. His presentation would have been more effective with an approach like this:

"This is a whistle. When you blow into it (he blows the whistle) it makes a very loud noise. If you ever find yourself pinned down in a foxhole, bullets whizzing over your head in every direction, take out this little jewel and blow hard. We'll come and try to get you out. Then maybe you'll live long enough to tell your grandchildren about being in the war."

Now that's the kind of solution-based approach anybody can understand. The first time around the sergeant told his audience a lot about what a whistle is and how it works, using a features-driven approach. But the second time he dramatically illustrated how it would solve a rather crucial problem, such as staying alive.

Sales representatives for Sabre Inc., one of the world's leading providers of technology for the travel industry, have discovered the benefits of using such solution-based approaches in their Advocating efforts. The software that Sabre sells, which enhances airline operations in areas such as yield management, crew management, flight operations, and scheduling, can be complex and often is highly customized to individual users. As a result, the software has a long list of important features.

So how do you decide what the customer needs to hear in a given sales presentation? "Before our sales reps attended the Counselor salesperson training course, they would go into a meeting and talk about all the different features a product had," says Jackie Friedman, director of Sabre's Sales Center of Excellence in Dallas, Texas. "But after they took the course, we found they were shortening the list of features they talked about to reflect the most important needs of the customer."

For example, the Sabre team was pitching a large Canadian travel agency it felt was a good candidate for a new software system that could take customer orders and bookings more quickly and efficiently than its current system. Before making a standardized presentation, however, one Sabre sales rep spent time talking to people who worked the front lines at the prospect company.

"Interestingly, he found that the front-line workers were frustrated because they had to re-enter customer data that the company already had in another database," says Friedman. "They thought it was a waste of time."

That was relevant because the Sabre system could read and write to multiple databases. "It's a minor feature that we might not even mention in a typical meeting with a prospect," says Friedman. "It's not critical to most people."

Yet by zeroing in on and uncovering a real problem, the Sabre rep illustrated that his product would save labor hours, prevent delays in customer service, and minimize errors from manually re-entering information. "We solved both fact and feeling concerns by focusing on one tiny aspect of our product," says Friedman. "And it was an easier sale for us, too. We didn't have to go through all the work of presenting a complete list of features and possible benefits because we could go right to the core problem and solve it."

You take a great risk in assuming your prospects will automatically translate product facts into people benefits. Professional persuading – what we call Advocating – starts when we begin interpreting, translating, and converting our features into people benefits.

The SAB Alternative

The sergeant's second attempt at "selling" the whistle follows the strategy we use when we become Advocates. First he presented the Solution (the whistle). Then he described the Advantage of his solution (we'll try to save you if you blow it when you're in danger). Finally, he illustrated the Benefits of the solution (you'll get to live to tell the tale). We call this the SAB approach. It's the shortest, straightest, and most persuasive path to helping a prospect believe in and buy your product.

You can use the SAB strategy for any product or service by following this three-step process:

Step 1: Explain your Solution in terms of its features. The solution could be an idea, a product or service, you (your Consultant Skills or industry knowledge, for example), or your company. Look at the main points of your Discovery Agreement and match your distinctive features to those points, but don't go overboard. There's a tendency to tell too much here. In this phase, the prospect only wants to know what time it is, not how the watch is made. Two fundamental questions should be answered for the prospect here: 1) What is the solution? 2) How does it function?

Step 2: The Advantage is how your solution addresses a cause and solves a problem. While the solution has to do with things, the advantage has to do with people – people getting their problems solved. The best way to communicate an advantage is to give a specific illustration or demonstration of the way a problem is solved, will be solved, or has been solved for oth-

Solution-Advantage-Benefit	
Solution:	What is it?
Advantage:	How does it solve the customer's problem?
Benefit:	What does it do for the customer?
	Answers the question, "So what?"

er clients. (We'll talk more about this later.) You'll probably spend more time and expend more words on the advantage than on the solution or even the benefit.

Step 3: The Benefit is the result of the solution and the advantage, and is *the feeling* the prospect has when a need has been satisfied. It's here where you explain how the product helps the prospect either *gain* or *maintain* the satisfaction of his or her needs.

There's a subtle but important difference between gaining and maintaining a sense of well being, and it's important you choose the right words to convey the separation. You show the *gained* benefits of your solution by using words or phrases such as winning, advancing, receiving credit, achieving, accomplishing a goal, receiving an honor, getting a bonus or promotion, being more successful, having a competitive edge, or enjoying the self-gratification of a job well done. You also illustrate gaining by showing how your product or service helps the customer to improve, increase, earn, return, add strength or opportunity, be more efficient or more productive, and gain time and money. The sergeant's Benefit (you'll get to tell your grandchildren because you survived) falls into the *gaining* category.

You help prospects understand how your offering *maintains* benefits by showing how it prevents feelings of being rejected, demoted, corrected, dismissed, embarrassed, blamed, chastised, or overlooked.

Benefits also are maintained when a product or service helps avoid waste, returns, lost time, and inefficiency.

The success of SAB is dependent on solution, advantage, and benefit being linked in a way the makes them appear as natural extensions of each other. Try asking yourself "so what?" after you've described a feature or an advantage. Is the feature mission-critical for the customer? You'll see why it's important to carry out the extension to include all three points of the SAB formula.

The Dangers of Fast-Forwarding Through Discovery

It is important, however, not to get ahead of yourself in using the SAB process. Solution-Advantage-Benefit Advocating is only effective when a consensus on your Discovery Agreement has been reached among key players in the client organization. If even one player on the decision-making team disagrees with your assessment, the sale could be lost. Even if reaching this consensus takes longer than hoped – even if it takes longer than the projected buying timeline given to you by the customer – it's crucial to persevere until it's achieved.

You can confirm consensus by asking a number of "checking" questions of all key players in the buying decision:

- "Is this a correct assessment of the situation in the company?" This is a good question to ask after you've summarized your understanding of the prospect's stated problems.
- "Is it fair to assume that you really need…?" Ask this question after the prospect has laid out specific needs like improved efficiency, less down time, and so on.
- "Did you say XYZ?" This clarifying question is especially important if prospects give concrete numbers that are substantially different from industry standards in areas like inventory volume, turnaround time, profit margins, etc.
- "So ABC is a primary objective, is that correct?" This question is important for potentially fuzzy or hard-to-quantify issues such as effi-

ciency, time savings, or productivity. If the customer can't quite quantify the problem, this question helps affirm that it is indeed a problem. Then you can provide the statistics, testimonials, or anecdotes to back it up, if necessary.

- "Has anything changed?" Even if you met two days ago, it's a good idea to make sure the situation as a whole is the same. A new CEO, a presidential election, or a shift in a remote region's foreign stock market can dramatically change a client's mindset about problems and needs. And if you know about it, there's at least the chance you can do something to keep the client on board.

To Advocate or Not to Advocate? It's the Prospect's Call

Many an enthusiastic salesperson has lost a good sale because he became an Advocate too early in the relationship, jumping to the pitch before conditions were right. This can lead a prospect to wonder, "How can he know this is the right product for me if he doesn't even know my business or unique requirements?" The more complex your product or service, the more tempting it is to jump in and say you have the perfect solution. Yet the easier it is for customers to pick that solution apart if you haven't done proper Discovery of their needs.

You'll know when the time is right for Advocating when some of the following situations occur:

- The customer says, "Let's get moving," or seems impatient when you talk about "further clarifying his needs."
- The customer mentions budgets, fiscal years, or other final monetary deadlines.
- The customer introduces you as a sales consultant to people you haven't met through the Discovery process.
- The customer tells you he has "narrowed the field."
- The customer says he is getting pressure "from above" to make a buying decision within a certain timeframe.

- "Would anyone in the company disagree with any of this?" If there's a possibility of disagreement, it's time to do some more homework or consensus building.
- "Does this seem to apply in your case?" This is a good question to ask one-on-one of key decision makers. Sometimes the answer will be "no," and then you'll need to find out why, and address the answer in your final presentation.

SECTION 2: THE ART OF THE SALES PRESENTATION

At this point you've interviewed all the key players and purchase influencers and have a good handle on concerns, needs, and personalities. You've researched the industry, the business, and put yourself in the prospect's shoes to make sure you haven't missed anything. You've synthesized all that information to create a Discovery Agreement and then built a compelling presentation tailored to those key issues or needs.

Yet just a few minutes into an SAB presentation, you see heads shaking and people whispering. You feel tension in the room. Someone may even get up and say, "I don't understand where you got the idea that that's a problem for us."

Whoa. You don't have total agreement. It can happen. But now what do you do? Try these steps:

1. If you know you have agreement from the majority of people in the room and only one or two people are dissenters, simply answer the question. Explain who supplied your information and how you analyzed it to come to that conclusion. Also mention people in the company you had review the Discovery Agreement before the presentation.

   Above all, avoid any hint of defensiveness. Don't let your body language, tone, or words say, "That's what I was told" or "Maybe you don't know your company as well you think you do."

In many cases you'll find the person with the concern isn't fully versed on the problem you're trying to solve or is testing you to see how much you really know about it. If you know the client as well as you should by this point, you'll have no trouble answering the question.

2. If it looks like a genuine disconnect between your information and the views of one or more people in the room, immediately stop the meeting. Apologize. Say you must have missed something when you interviewed the many people you talked to about this. Ask if there are any others you might interview to get more or different information. Yes, there is a slight chance you'll lose the sale at this point, but if you've created a high level of trust between yourself and the client, it's still salvageable.

3. Set a meeting with your key contact, who should be familiar with the Discovery Agreement presented in the meeting. Ask him or her for candid input on what went wrong. Is there a new personality in the group? New dynamics in the company? Are people changing their minds, afraid to admit problems when they're sitting next to the CEO or senior vice president in a meeting, but showing no such hesitation when interviewed by you one-on-one? Is someone testing you or playing "devil's advocate"? Did you really misunderstand something? Did something major happen in the world, the industry, or within the company during the last few days that could affect the sale?

4. If there was a misunderstanding or a mistake on your part, redraft the Discovery Agreement and present it to your key contact as well as to the person or persons who pointed the problem out. *Do not* explain how you got the wrong impression or who gave you the wrong information. If you didn't fully understand the situation the first time around, admit that, but never blame the situation on someone else, regardless of how at fault they may be. You'll be surprised at how much credibility you gain by facing the situation and moving forward.

Adapting Your Advocating Strategy to Role Players

Each decision-maker or purchase influencer involved in a buying decision has his own *personal* agenda and *task* agenda, the various motives, desires, and triggers that can differ wildly from person to person. Salespeople who take the time to decipher these agendas can adapt their Solution-Advantage-Benefit presentations accordingly, greatly increasing their odds of closing a sale. Of course, the skill of reading these types is worthy of another whole book – or more – but some generalized portraits will get you started.

Here's one way to classify these decision-makers or influencers:

The Economic Buyer. This is the person who ultimately controls the purse strings, but very often it's not the contact with whom you spend the most time. This person is concerned with the "bigger picture" and is mainly interested in the results and benefits of the contemplated purchase. A statement like this sums up the attitude of the Economic Buyer:

> *"I understand the problem and know we need to buy a new telecommunications system. But that's just one of the many problems I have. I can't afford to meddle in all of them. I have other capable people to do that for me. All I want to do is take a quick look at the solution they come up with and decide whether I feel like spending our money on it or not."*

The Gatekeeper. This person often has no real authority in the buying decision, but controls access to those who do. He or she is the principal contact, the coordinator and the one who can open the door to all the rest. Secretaries, administrative assistants, and purchasing agents often play this role. The Gatekeepers also have to be sold, but it's a mistake to rest one's case with them and not take it to the real decision makers. The Gatekeeper's attitude is expressed like this:

"Since news of the search for a better telecommunications system was announced, I've literally been besieged by vendors. It's my job to find, filter, and funnel the good ones to the proper people. I, of course, won't make the final decision. But I do have a lot to say about which one is recommended."

The Concept Buyer. In some cases the impetus to consider new products or services comes from someone remote from day-to-day operations. It might, for example, be a staff officer who passes on a good idea to a line manager. He or she is like a godparent to the purchase, someone whose blessings you'll likely need before a final decision is made. From the Concept Buyer you might hear:

"Sometimes it takes a detached, impartial observer like myself to see a need and identify the problem. In this case, it's a question of instigating some action. It can take months to get any news from here to there or even longer from hither to yon. Thanks to me, the Economic Buyer has taken some steps. And naturally, before he buys, he'll ask me if I find it suitable."

The Feasibility Buyer. This person examines the specific merits and demerits of your solution – the one who looks at all the pros and cons. He or she is also the resident comparison shopper, the one who weighs your product or service against the competition's offerings. The concern of this buyer is usually quality and output. The Feasibility Buyer might express his or her attitude like this:

"I talk to certain, selected vendors referred to me by the Gatekeeper. I weigh their proposals, evaluate them, and look at all the alternatives from the standpoint of practicality. Currently I am favoring the most expensive model. It has the latest features that will help us boost productivity and reduce costs over the long-term."

The Budget Director. Almost always, there is someone around who "puts the pencil" to the proposed solution. This person raises the financial questions regarding price, placement in the budget, options to lease and methods of financing. This person must be sold on the economic soundness of a decision. The following sums up the attitude of the Budget Director:

> *"Latest features indeed. Bah! Altogether too costly. We would need to buy everything new. Establish comprehensive training programs. Heavy start-up costs. Money doesn't grow on trees, you know. What's wrong with last year's ? I hear the other vendor offers a discount on it."*

The End User. This person or group has to live with whatever is purchased. These are the people who will actually use or work with the new product or service. They may not have the authority to decide, but if they don't like the product, they can create powerful resistance and block the sale. The attitude of the End User is:

> *"Let them talk all they want. But they had better get my opinion before making any rash decisions. After all, I'm the one who has to make this new telecommunications system work. And frankly, I don't think anything will ever replace the system I've perfected and gotten used to."*

In some selling situations, only two or three of the role players listed above may be involved, while in other cases all of these – and more – will have some say. Each role-player will have a different point of view on the problem and its origins, not to mention which solution they think is best.

Others will have multiple roles. For example, a manager buying a new laptop computer for her own use might play the dual roles of End User and Budget Director. She might also be a Feasibility Buyer. Roles also can change depending on the product or service being considered. For example, the IT manager may be the Budget Director for the purchase of new servers, the End User for a new training program, the Feasibility Buyer for a new accounting software program, the Concept Buyer for a satellite communications system, and the Economic Buyer for software upgrades. Many companies make a point of having cross-functional bying teams, and that significantly compounds the multiple role issues.

A good way to make sure you address each of these roles is to answer the following questions:

- Who are all the people involved in the decision-making process?
- What is each one's role?
- Who has the most impact? The next most?
- How do they relate to each other on the organizational chart?
- How do they relate to each other informally?
- What is each one's perceived personal agenda, based on their personality style and other clues?
- How will a favorable decision help or hurt this person?
- If I don't know these things, how can I find out?

Based on the answers, develop a strategic advocating plan that answers these questions:

- Can I influence the role or impact of any of these people? Using what specific tactics?
- In what order should I present to them? Together? Who first? Who last?
- Can I add favorable parties or even subtract unfavorable ones?

The salesperson who finally makes the sale is the one who can best resolve the differing viewpoints, reduce the tension, and manage the necessary compromises between all these different role players.

Winning the Day Before the Day

Preparation. Preparation. Preparation. There's rarely too much of it when it comes to effective sales presentations. But how you choose to use that preparation time makes all the difference between closing a deal and going home without a payoff for your hard work.

Preparation for important presentations should focus not only on what you're going to say, but also to whom, when, and in what surroundings. Sometimes there is little you can do to affect the latter variables. But often you have more control than you think when it comes to arranging things to your advantage. Consider these ideas:

- Set up advance presentations. When making group presentations, attempt to set up advance, informal, individual meetings with some of the key participants. This strategy offers two benefits. One, it gives you a chance to double-check and expand your understanding of the problem to be solved. Two, it provides a forum to test the acceptability of some of the ideas you're planning to propose.
These advance meetings also give you a chance to smoke out objections before they pop up at a final meeting. That way you can prepare for them in advance rather than being forced into impromptu and possibly inadequate responses in the middle of your final presentation.
- Lobby for internal advocates. Advance meetings also help to pre-sell some of the decision-makers and create internal advocates. At the same time, while you don't have final say in who will attend your presentation, it doesn't hurt to ask to have someone there who you know is in your corner.

If you know that Barbara is your "internal advocate," the one who really feels the fever and believes in your proposed solutions, propose something along these lines: "Dave, I was just wondering if Barbara is going to be in on this presentation. She's already provided a lot of the background data on the problem, and I think she could be very helpful." Your internal advocate is a surrogate salesperson and because of his or her unique position (being "of the company") is likely to provide support that will have high credibility with other members of the group.

- Expert witnesses. It helps to bring along your own support personnel, your technical specialists, your sales manager, or sometimes even a trusted consultant or subcontractor. You can turn to them as "expert witnesses" in areas where your own back-wheel (technical) knowledge is thin. Also, as knowledgeable observers looking in on your presentation, they'll often know when you've missed a key presentation point. They'll have the competence to supply it or to illustrate other advantages and benefits they sense are important to prospects.
- Research participants. You've heard it before, but you need quality information – some might say intelligence – on who will be there, which roles they play, and what agendas they bring to the buying process. If there are participants you haven't met, first do some relationship building to establish credibility. Review your material for currency, especially the Discovery Agreement.
- Your own turf. Giving a presentation on your own premises, while not always possible, can prove a powerful advantage. In your own plant, conference room, or offices, all the resources you might need are at your fingertips, and your comfort level likely is higher.

If what you're selling is high-tech manufacturing equipment, for instance, you could conduct a plant tour or walk-through of your facilities. You can *show*, in depth, as well as tell your story. You can be confident of having an adequate meeting room. You have more control over possible distractions. You have greater freedom in your choice and use of multimedia sales aids.

What about when the meeting must take place on the prospect's premises? You can at least tactfully let the prospect know what you'd like to have. For example:

> *"George, it looks like there's going to be at least eight people at the meeting. And what I'd really like to do is show them a short videotape of some applications like the one you're considering. So do you think it would be possible to get that conference room we were in the other day?"*

It's unlikely that George or any other prospect would take umbrage at such a suggestion. After all, that meeting must be of value to George and his people too, or they wouldn't be letting you make your presentation in the first place.

- Documentation. Prepare a written proposal or summary of your presentation and Discovery Agreement to hand out to participants during or after the meeting. After you've left, the prospects will probably hold their own meeting to evaluate your presentation – and the written document will help them recall the major advantages and benefits of your solution accurately and in the most favorable light. Make this document as impressive as possible – well organized, well written, tailor-made, and in a bound volume.
- Have a Plan B. Whether you're making a one-on-one presentation or selling to a group, it's always wise to have an optional proposal to present. In computer equipment sales, for example, the sales proposal frequently offers options of purchasing or renting equipment, purchasing technical support in lump sum or by the hour, and various installation options.

Harvey Mackay, the business-book author, speaker, and envelope manufacturer, carries different sales proposals in different jacket pockets. Then, as a meeting wears on and he gets a better feel for where his prospect is leaning, he pulls out the "perfect" proposal. Having a good Discovery Agreement can prevent this level of suspense. But it's also unlikely your proposed solution – following Murphy's Law – will run the gamut of prospect scrutiny without at least some modification to its makeup, the purchase terms, the implementation plan, or other factors.

When prospects disagree with some part of your solution, they may not suggest an alternative of their own. They'll be looking to you to supply the options, so it pays to think them out in advance and get them down on paper.

Gathering Competitive Intelligence

You sell high-end technical solutions to a very tight-knit industry. You can count your potential clients on two hands. You can count your competitors on one hand. And all of your products are essentially the same, give or take a few bells and whistles or points of emphasis. So how do you provide a clear distinction between your offering and the competition's?

Competitive positioning, once the domain of the marketing department, has become far more critical in person-to-person selling. While your company or sales manager will probably lead the way, there's much you can do on your own to get an accurate sense of the competition's latest moves. Try these tactics:

- Ask your customer. If you've developed a trusting relationship, your customer might hand over the competitors' sales sheets, pricing literature, or other information. At a minimum, the customer may tell you the high points of the competitors' products as they were presented to him.

  It also pays to ask the customer who he thinks the chief competition is. In today's fast moving, saturated markets, he may point in a different direction than the one you anticipated. You may learn about a new entrant or about a new strategy from an entrenched player.

- Share information with each other. Encourage your organization to create space on a corporate intranet for sharing competitive intelligence and to reward sales reps that regularly post information there. Make sure they have clear guidelines that help separate valuable contributions from trivial details.

- Meet the people. In addition to attending industry events, join an industry sales organization. In the pharmaceutical industry, for example, many salespeople in major cities meet monthly to discuss issues. While your peers or rivals won't freely give away their positioning, a few stray words here or insinuations there can provide some clue.
- Search the literature. You're already perusing the trade magazines, financial papers, and online sites to stay up on your industry or niche. These resources also can be a fair source of competitive information. Look for the competition's ads, and don't forget to access the competition's web site periodically for clues about new strategic direction, pricing changes, product, or other useful news.
- Look to new employees. Employees fresh out of school may have done in-depth case studies on the competition. Others may be new arrivals from a competitor's pool. Don't just concentrate on the sales staff. Marketing, accounting, and even clerical staff often have unique insights into their former employers. But respect ethical boundaries by not requesting confidential information.

How "Word Laziness" Can Cost You Sales

The natural result of communication is misunderstanding.
If you really want to be understood, you've got to work at it.

Dr. George Shapiro, Professor Emeritus of Speech Communication at the University of Minnesota, has studied theories of communication for decades, and he knows the power of words to make a point with his own university students. Yet Shapiro also knows that words can be barriers to effective communication. The problem, he notes, is that words are not actual *things*. They only represent things. They're symbols of things. And the same symbols can mean vastly different things to different people.

For example, a flag is a symbol of a country, not the country itself. Yet think of the different things people attach to the symbol of their flag. People say they will die for the flag. Many countries consider it a crime to burn their national flag. At the same time, when you say the word "flag" to a multinational group, every individual in the room will see a different picture. And that's a concrete object. Think what happens when you start talking with prospects about intangible items such as *support, efficiency, reliability,* or *trust.*

When a word symbol is used, each of us creates a different word image in our mind of what the symbol represents. These images are a reflection of our own personal experiences. And these differences represent one of the major roadblocks to effective communication.

Helping prospects intellectually understand your solution is one thing – it's what you might call the science of selling. Helping them visualize and get a visceral "feel" for the benefits of having their problem solved, that's where the art comes in. Salespeople have to be experts not only at shaping the solution message, but also at communicating it.

To that end, it helps to keep your Advocating statements – and the words within them – simple, familiar, and dramatic. Following these guidelines will help:

- Get over the notion that the more complicated you make your presentation sound, the more impressed your prospects will be. When sales reps are unsure of themselves, they often try to dazzle listeners by using big words or a technical vocabulary. But that usually backfires, confusing and irritating prospects rather than impressing them. Whenever possible, present your story in your prospect's language. Remember, your job is to persuade. That will be a lot easier if you learn the prospect's language instead of asking him or her to learn yours.
- Avoid abstract words. Abstract words are difficult to visualize or to relate to experience. Check your presentations for abstract-speak.

Are your words concrete, simple, and easy-to-understand? Word pictures help move an abstract idea closer to the real thing and can move a prospect a giant step closer to understanding the real meaning of your solution.

- Show rather than tell. Prospects get the picture more quickly if you show your product in action rather than just describe it. No wonder so many salespeople are still willing to lug around heavy sample cases, and so many businesses use the "test drive" to give customers a hands-on feel for products they're considering. Nothing communicates better than the real thing, even in this age of Internet-based purchasing.

But when you don't have the real thing, what then? You already know the answer to that one. Some sort of visual aid, whether it's a realistic demo on a Web site or an aid that can be used in face-to-face selling. A PowerPoint presentation, models, brochures, charts, anything you can combine with words will help a prospect experience what your product or service can do. Research into adult learning shows that understanding and information retention can increase dramatically when an individual is allowed to touch, feel, and play with a product. It's a persuasive tool.

- Choose your analogies carefully. If your solution is complex or intangible, you can bring it to life by likening it to something concrete or widely known – in other words, by using an analogy.

Life insurance agents have long used the "marble" analogy to demonstrate how premium payments can get larger and heavier the longer a prospect waits to purchase a needed insurance policy. The analogy goes like this: "Mr. Prospect, if I gave you a marble to put in your pocket and you have carry that around with you the rest of your life, that would be a little inconvenient. If I gave you a baseball to carry around with you, well, you could probably manage that too, even though it would be a bother. But if I gave you a basketball to carry around the rest of your life, the inconvenience and trouble would almost drive you crazy.

"Well, when you buy this policy, even though you may feel that it's more than you need right now, it will be like that marble – a little inconvenient, but that's all. But if you wait and grow older, I'd have to come back to you with a baseball. If you wait too long or your health goes bad, it may have to be a basketball. What would you think of making it easy on yourself by letting the marble solve your problem right now?"

- Compare and contrast. Most solutions become more meaningful if we compare and contrast them to something familiar. Then it's easier for prospects to see how they're different and better.

While many sales reps like to do this with competitive products, they often can do it just as effectively with their own products. Consider the challenge of trying to get customers to buy an expensive software upgrade when they feel the old version is meeting their current needs just fine. Yet if you stage a hands-on demonstration showing how the new version handles common work tasks with greater ease or efficiency than the old, you can win converts.

The Third-Party Story: The Ultimate Illustrator

Nothing more vividly illustrates the human experience of having a problem solved than the third-party story. As they listen to what happened to someone else in a similar situation, prospects identify with the character and empathize with the event. They have the same experience vicariously. The third-party story has more built-in believability and credibility than much of what you can do or say yourself. You are, after all, talking about a real problem with real results experienced by real people, not a "what-if" scenario based on hypotheticals or your own proclamations about the power of your product.

Compare the relative persuasive power of these two statements by a computer software salesperson:

"If you do a lot of word processing, this software is the best there is. It has easy pull-down menus for formatting, plenty of embedded help features, some innovative new shortcuts, and it's easy to learn."

That sounds okay. After all, easy to use and learn are important selling features. But let's give him another chance:

"One of my customers at Mega Corp, Bridget Jones, came into work one day to find her computer stolen. It was devastating, but to top it off she had a big report due that next day. The information technology department was able to set her up with a new computer for the time being. The problem was it didn't have the same word processing software she was used to. She was panicked, but she says it took her about 10 minutes to get the hang of our new software. It's very intuitive. Her report was delivered on time and formatted beautifully. Ever since then, she's used our software."

The first version was an endorsement and recommendation. The second was an endorsement and dramatized *illustration*. The latter was interesting and more believable because it dramatized the solution, advantage, and benefit.

Drama in selling tends to be much misunderstood. When we suggest you add some drama to your presentation, we're not suggesting you become theatrical. If you do that, you will probably become less believable. Instead, we're suggesting that, when appropriate, you say what you were going to say anyway in a more human and interesting way.

Ingredients of Good Third-Party Stories

Good third-party stories don't happen by accident. They're planned.

And if they're really good, it's because they've been prepared and practiced in advance. How many good third-party stories do you have in your repertoire? If the answer is "not nearly as many as I'd like," perhaps it's time to build a few by reviewing your list of satisfied customers. Select a few of the most interesting cases, talk briefly again to some of the people involved, and take notes to gather some favorable quotes. Just make sure you get permission to use their real names and experiences and that you keep third-party stories updated or fresh, not perpetually recycled.

Good third-party stories are very simple. They aren't complicated, and they don't go into irrelevant detail. Use this outline to create them and you'll have all the elements you need:

1. *Describe the third party with a problem similar to the one your prospect is facing.* Ideally it's someone the prospect respects or can identify with. Think of this as the conflict built into a good drama. Use one or two sentences to explain what the problem was and why it was important to this person or his company. ("Your situation reminds me a lot of...")

2. *Describe the solution you and the third party tried.* Discard details of the decision-making process and jump straight to implementation. Emphasize the buyer's decision to buy rather than your role in recommending the solution.

3. *Describe the advantage or benefit.* What happened when the product or service was up and running? How long did it take to make an impact? What were some of the lasting benefits?

4. *Describe how the third party felt.* You won't always have this information, but you should be able to imagine it. Look for words such as relieved, satisfied, and happy when you interview the customer for a case study. In this last section of a good third-party story, he or she can easily say:
   - "It made my life easier."
   - "It made my job more interesting."

- "The new efficiency/cost control/revenues contributed to my promotion."
- "It got those guys in the other department off my back."
- "The operators are happier and customer complaints are down at least 50 percent."

SECTION 3: HANDLING OBJECTIONS AND CLOSING

You've kept a prospect closely involved in developing and reviewing a Discovery Agreement, but now that you've entered the Advocating stage, it's time for things to shift back squarely into your court, right? Wrong. You've worked hard to develop rapport with the buyer, and this is no time to return to a lone-wolf act. Getting involvement from buyers at strategic points throughout the process of Counselor selling, including the all-important presentation, can set up a series of "minor closes" that lead to agreement on the whole. Such participation can:

- Help buyers feel responsible for solving their own problems.
- Help you know whether you're on target in the early stages of crafting a presentation.
- Build agreement one step at a time.
- Gradually get buyers on your side before a final close. Getting them to make a series of small commitments makes it easier to get the big one at the end of the process. In most complex sales, a series of agreements are reached before contracts are signed or money ever changes hands.
- Clarify a gap or misunderstanding in a Discovery Agreement.
- Provide opportunities to deal with objections before formally asking for the business.

Some key points at which to keep buyers involved include:

1. After reviewing the Discovery Agreement. Does the buyer agree

with the specific problems for which you're presenting a solution? Also, new players may have joined the game since the Discovering stage. You won't be able to address their unique concerns or needs unless you review the Discovery Agreement with them.

2. While presenting Solution-Advantage-Benefit statements. Does the buyer understand the solution? Does the buyer see the advantage as helpful in addressing task or personal motives?

3. After the presentation. Does the buyer agree with your recommendations?

There is a point at which the buyer can be *too* involved, however, and you'll want to avoid crossing that line. It's important you see buyer participation as a guide, not an interruption or loss of control. Buyer participation may be excessive if:

1. The buyer wants to help write the sales proposal.

2. A buyer wants access to proprietary information about your company's pricing, product differentiation, or services.

3. A buyer starts resenting the time you're asking of her, hinting that this work is *your* job, not hers.

4. The buyer seems to have lost some objectivity in the eyes of superiors, appearing to function more as part of your "team" than representing the best interests of her company. Buyers can be oblivious to this perception, so it's important that you gently point out the importance of appearing impartial and businesslike during the decision-making process. Since you often have to persuade more than one decision-maker, it's key that all perceive your solution as the best of the lot based on business criteria, not just on the quality of established personal relationships.

Using the Assumptive Close

You have an excellent, well-researched Discovery Agreement. Your prospect agrees your solution is a good match for his needs. In other words, it's a perfect situation for "assumptive closing." The Assumptive Close is asking for the order in a way that assumes the prospect has decided to buy instead of asking *if* he wants to buy. So instead of asking the customer if he wants to buy, you ask him *how he wants to buy*.

You'll know you've reached this point because asking for the sale will feel easy and natural. You will probably be thinking, "Okay, there's nothing else I can think of to do. We've worked a long time on this, covering all the angles and hitting all the right steps. Of course he's going to buy." Not asking for the order at this point would feel unnatural or illogical.

The Assumptive Close is based on offering the prospect options. Not stark, tension-raising options such as "take it or leave it," but options such as a choice between certain details outlined in your solution. This makes you "easy to buy from."

For example, when the new owners of a cocker spaniel took the dog to the veterinarian for the first time, they were offered several payment options that included four different levels of pet insurance. The owners felt they might not need the insurance. But after a short, informative presentation by a veterinary assistant, it became clear that the question they needed to answer was "which one?" not "insurance or no insurance?".

Or consider this example of an assumptive close:

> *"So, to summarize, this configuration of equipment will solve your billing cycle problem. Now I guess the question is whether we go with the turnkey approach or we have your own people do part of the equipment installation. Which way do you think we should go?"*

The Assumptive Close doesn't have to happen at the end of the sales process. It's also effective when used to ask permission to proceed to the next step in a sales process. You can use it to propose a trial run, a large-group presentation, or permission to conduct a study, for example.

Choosing to use an Assumptive Close is only step one. You also have to know which type of Assumptive Close is best for your prospect, your own personality and the unique sales situation. Here are six options. You may already know some or all of them by different names:

- The Mini-Max. This is a way of minimizing the potential downside of a purchase decision and emphasizing the possibility of gain. "The worst that could happen is... On the other hand, the benefit is..." This works especially well with skittish buyers looking for an extra dose of reassurance and confirmation that their decision is right.
- The Balance Sheet (or pros and cons) close. The balance sheet is a way of looking at reasons for and against a purchase and letting the facts speak for themselves. Make two lists that detail the pros and cons of purchasing your product or service. Realistically, all the topics won't have a counterbalancing weight. For example, "a savings of one million Euros in the next year" probably won't be overshadowed by "several weeks of 10 percent underproduction as employees learn the new system."

If there are more reasons for than against, simply ask the buyer which side weighs heavier for going forward. If there are more reasons against, you have objections that are still questions in the buyer's mind. You need to resolve these concerns and obtain the prospect's agreement that they can be erased from the "cons" side of the worksheet.

This close works well with buyers who want assurances they're making the right decision, in part by showing the risks of *not* buying. It's also helpful for showing buyers how their decision to go ahead can result in new respect or standing within their organizations.

- Cost Analysis. This is a way of examining the value gained for the price paid. List the cost of your solution. Then weigh the consequences of both implementing and not implementing the solution in terms of money saved, hours reduced, percentage of increased productivity, or other tangible outcomes of your solution. This approach works well with buyers who demand hard evidence and proof that committing to your solution is justified.

- Options. This gives the buyer a greater sense of control over the buying decision by asking which of several options he or she prefers. You probably have narrowed the choices to a small pool so you might offer the option, for example, of an extended service contract, installation, or minor product features. You might ask "Which of these do you prefer?" or "How many would you like to start with?" as a way of creating options.

- The Next Step. Rather than asking outright for the order, simply ask if you should "call the installation team to set up a meeting with the client" or if you can "work with accounts payable for a financing strategy." By committing to this next step, the customer is actually committing to buy.

- Summing up. This low-pressure close is especially effective if you don't have clear options to present. Simply provide a summary of your Discovery Agreement featuring the problem-solution benefits of the recommended product. For example: "Based on what you said about the lighter weight reducing your shipping costs, I'd like to suggest an initial order of 200,000 Class Two containers. What do you think?"

Managing Your Fears About Closing

If your own daily experiences haven't yet confirmed it, chances are they soon will: Sales is among the most stressful jobs in the developed world. Rejection plays a recurring role, and there's little feeling of closure, since there's always tomorrow and a new quota to be met.

Those who endure and succeed in the profession find healthy and proactive ways to cope with the fear, rather than pretending it doesn't exist, says John Boettcher, an industrial psychologist based in Dallas, Texas. One of the biggest fears for new salespeople is the close, or the point in the Advocating process where they ask for the business. New salespeople often miss prime opportunities to ask for business because they feel they're imposing on a buyer, or that if they don't ask, they can't be turned down.

While it can be difficult to overcome this fear, you can teach yourself to manage it in a way that actually fuels your closing success, Boettcher says. And the more skillful you become at asking for the order, the less you'll fear it.

These ideas can help manage your anxiety over closing:

1. Consciously monitor your own fears and what you say to yourself about asking for business. "Even top salespeople will say things like, 'I probably won't get this account' or 'I just hate this part of the sales cycle,'" says Boettcher. "Recognize that it's completely natural to be fearful of rejection and then go from there." In fact, he says, you should be concerned if some fear doesn't exist.

2. Recognize that you're one of millions. Talk to other salespeople about their fears, and you'll find you're not alone. "There's an unwritten rule that good salespeople don't talk about their fears, but that's ridiculous," says Boettcher. "People at the top of any field have had to overcome a lot to get there. Many are just waiting for you to ask their advice."

3. Challenge yourself to re-label thoughts. Re-label your negative thoughts about closing to be more positive, and then move on. Thomas Edison was once asked how he was able to persevere after over a thousand failures in creating the light bulb. His answer was, "I did not fail a thousand times. I succeeded, and success involved 1,001 steps." Rather than focus on the "make or break" close, focus on the successful completion of the previous steps. Larry Wilson, founder of Wilson Learning Worldwide, said many years ago.

"Don't think of it as nine rejections before making a single sale. The previous nine are just steps to a goal." In other words, if you believe it takes nine "no's" to get to a "yes," those no's will feel like natural steps toward an objective, not continual slaps in the face.

4. Separate yourself from your job. "It's important you understand rejection of your product isn't rejection of you," says Boettcher. "Think of rejection as a natural part of the job. Nurses get sore feet. Accountants get sore eyes. Salespeople get rejected. If you've done the job well up to this point, you have earned the right to ask for the business."

5. Focus on what you do like. Okay, so you don't like to ask for the business. We all have parts of our jobs we don't like. Just do it and move on, Boettcher suggests. "Throw yourself into the parts of the job you do like. Do you like the analysis of the client's situation? Then work to analyze exactly how to perform the best close for that client. Actually doing it will seem natural when the time comes."

6. Remember that the client is expecting the close. Clients aren't naïve; they understand they're in the middle of a sales process. They expect the close. They are waiting for you to ask for the business. So do it. Don't leave them in suspense.

7. You've earned the right. You've worked hard in the Relating, Discovering, and initial Advocating steps, so you've earned the right to ask for the business. Why? Because you thoroughly understand the buyer's situation and have recommended a solution that will help him solve an important need.

8. Reward yourself. Whether you landed the account or not, if your close was good you should give yourself a pat on the back, says Boettcher. "Reward yourself for a job well done. Don't necessarily tie it to getting the sale."

The LSCPA Model: Understanding Objections to Death

Of course, an airtight Discovery Agreement and deftly used Assumptive Close are no guarantee of an all-important purchase order being signed. When it comes to sales negotiations, the unexpected, untimely, and just plain bizarre objection can emerge at any time, threatening to derail all your hard work and efforts. Next to asking for the order, dealing with objections is the most feared part of a salesperson's job.

Yet most successful salespeople see objections as opportunities rather than harbingers of doom. They can manifest hidden or previously squelched concerns and offer another chance to deal with them. "I rarely worry about a clear objection, and I don't even worry much if a client is yelling at me," says Pat Carey, the IBM sales rep. "What I do worry about is the client who is quiet and just fades away. If there's a real objection, there's a real opportunity."

By adopting such a problem-solving mindset, you not only stand a better chance of overcoming objections, you can develop even greater rapport with prospects. When many conventional salespeople encounter real objections late in a sales cycle, their first instinct isn't to explore further or clarify the objection, but to push harder what they've already recommended.

For example, if a prospect objects based on price, the conventional salesperson might react by pushing value – the benefits a prospect receives for that higher price – only this time with greater emphasis or from a different angle. The Counselor salesperson, on the other hand, returns to the Discovery process to find out more about that price objection. Is the objection a value or budget issue, for example? If it's a budget issue – if the funds truly aren't there to buy at the negotiated price – it may be a deal breaker, and you may have the wrong solution for the prospect. It's important to know the real motives behind objections so you can adjust accordingly.

One proven way to deal successfully with objections is by using the LSCPA model. The letters stand for **Listen-Share-Clarify-Problem Solve-Action**. It's an approach recommended by mental health professionals as well as sales experts for dealing with objections and conflict in business and personal arenas.

Listen: Encourage buyers to talk openly about any lingering concerns. "Listen until they have completely drained themselves," suggests Keith Sondrall. "The buyer is in no frame of mind to listen to a logical clarification or solution until his or her tension is reduced, so keep listening even when they stop talking. Listen to their eyes. Listen to the way they look at you and the way they shuffle the papers on their desks."

The true power of listening at this stage comes in the simple acknowledgment of concerns, Sondrall says. "There are always several sides to an issue, and the buyer knows that as well as you do," he says. "They just want to make sure you know their side completely. You are listening to honor their feelings, not to make a point about the facts of the situation."

Share: "Share the buyer's concerns without judging them," says Sondrall. You want to show that you understand and respect their *perception* of the problem, even if that perception doesn't necessarily square with your own. Useful phrases here include "I can understand why you'd feel that way," "You seem to feel strongly about that" and "You're right."

Avoid arguing with the buyer's perceptions at all costs. It's hard to calm someone's emotions by engaging in debate. The goal here is to return them to a reasonable state so you can begin to solve the problem.

Clarify: In more cases than not, the concern the buyer brings up is not the real problem. There will be times, for instance, when the real problem is within the buyer's own organization, and he or she is "dumping" on you because you're a convenient target. "Your objective should be to get to the root of the problem," says Sondrall. "Is it really that your product is too expensive, or is it that the client's management has suddenly applied new criteria to the buying decision near the conclusion of the purchase process?"

You can clarify buyers' real objections or concerns in one of the following ways:

- Restate the problem in your own words and ask checking questions to find out if you've understood what the buyer means.
- Turn the objection into a question.
- Ask more fact-finding and feeling-finding questions (see page 49 for examples of these).

If you find that the root problem is different from what the buyer was first talking about, return to the Listen stage and proceed from there. "I know situations where it took three or four passes through the listening, sharing, and clarifying stages before the salesperson got to the real heart of the problem," says Sondrall. "Some prospects don't understand what the real problem is themselves, and the questioning process helps them flesh it out. Others are just embarrassed to admit it's an internal problem at first."

Jonathon Smythe understands how things can go awry late in a sales cycle. A sales representative for Medtronic, the multinational medical device manufacturer, Smythe was convinced that a large hospital was going to make a significant purchase of Medtronic heart pacemakers. Yet when he arrived at the meeting he thought was a mere formality to close the deal, he was met with an alarming objection. "The key decision maker said it would take too long and be too expensive to train the physicians to use the new device when the one they were currently using was just fine," Smythe remembers. "I was dumbfounded. I remember thinking, 'Where did that come from after all this time?'"

Rather than showing his concern or getting defensive, Smythe listened and empathized with the problem. "I asked a number of clarifying questions, and it turned out the real problem was a new internal purchasing procedure that had to include the training costs as part of the budget for the new item. On top of it, the client was being evaluated on sticking to the budget, as well as on making next year's product buying decisions within a couple weeks. He was frustrated and a bit scared," says Smythe.

Using the LSCPA process, Smythe was able to walk the buyer back through the proposed deal to calm fears about exorbitant training time or costs. This required Smythe to analyze, be creative, and ultimately to defuse the unexpected tension. "Then I showed the customer how much his business really meant to me by turning his proposal around in a very short time frame," he says. "I got that particular business, but I also got tremendous customer loyalty."

Problem Solve: Once you fully understand the objection, handle the situation as if you have a new, bite-sized Discovery Agreement, says Sondrall. "Start thinking of solutions, and invite the customer to help you brainstorm. Bring up examples of how you've solved similar problems with other customers. Think of this as a small sale within your larger sale."

Say, for example, you sell manufacturing inputs such as raw chemicals and you have an existing customer who is complaining about your delivery support. He was told he could have product delivered within 24 hours. But twice in the first month of your relationship the deliveries took between 48 and 72 hours. He's irate. How should you problem solve?

First, check with your own people. What are the issues from their perspective? Has the customer been ordering larger amounts than he had planned? Has he been asking for weekend or holiday delivery? Has your company had cutbacks in delivery service? Do you use a third-party delivery service? Are the orders not getting to the delivery people quickly enough?

Let's say it's a problem that can't be resolved from your end. Perhaps the customer has just acquired a new site that is outside of your normal 24-hour delivery zone. You can't provide the service the customer wants but you *can* help solve his problem.

Start by asking him questions about his need for product on such short notice.

For example:

- Is it a warehousing issue? Does the customer not have the warehouse space on site to keep a reasonable supply of your product? If that's the case, you might help locate an inexpensive warehouse near his facility. Or, you might mention that another client stored the product at its central facility and relied on an overnight service to deliver it to customers. To make this solution more amenable, you might reintroduce your bulk purchase prices.

- Is it an accounting issue? Some accounting systems require the internal department to "pay" for the product when it's received instead of prorating bulk shipments over several months. Depending on the time of year, this can wreck havoc on some managers' budgets. If your client is in this situation, perhaps there is a method of determining how much product is needed 72 hours in advance instead of 24. You might mention that one company in the same situation discovered, after further investigation, that it was a staffing issue – no one was free to check on the supply until the need became urgent. You might solve that by having someone from your ordering department make a call once a week to check on the supply for the client.

- Is it a liability issue? Perhaps the product is very volatile or potentially dangerous, and the client's risk management department simply doesn't want more of it in the warehouse than is necessary. Again, brainstorm ways to work with the 72-hour delivery as opposed to the 24-hour delivery.

- Do the needs fluctuate wildly? Some manufacturing operations literally don't know what they will be working on until 24 hours ahead of time. If that's the case, perhaps you can work out what a three-day supply of the product would be and ensure it's always kept in the customer's warehouse. The customer then calls to replenish that order as soon as it's being used.

Ask for Action: The final step in LSCPA is getting feedback from the buyer regarding your proposed solution to their objection and then asking for some action. Says Sondrall: "Now that you're back in the sales process, you know the next step: Use an Assumptive Close to resolve the objection."

All of the Assumptive Close techniques mentioned earlier in this chapter work well, he says, depending on your personality and the type of objection involved. But be sure to include these tactics when asking for action:

- Ask prospects to recognize what happened. "I like to ask them to do me a favor next time and tell me the real problem upfront so we can work it out faster," says Sondrall. "After all, we've built a strong, trusting relationship, and we both share responsibility for making the deal work."
- Set a deadline. Dealing with objections represents a minor change to the sales plan so they need to be treated expeditiously, if possible. "Commit to a date and time that you'll have an answer or a rewritten proposal, then proceed to the next step, whether it's a presentation or an Assumptive Close," Sondrall says.
- Don't take no for an answer. "If the buyer is reluctant to commit, there is probably another problem under the surface. You'll need to return to the Clarifying stage and work the process again," says Sondrall.

Handling the Complex Objection

While it may feel like the LSCPA process can be accomplished at one meeting, many objections take a long time to resolve, especially if they're complex and involve more than one person in the buying decision.

In some cases you'll find the person making the objection doesn't even know all the underlying concerns, is objecting based on an incomplete picture of the situation or is simply making a power play. Here are some tactics to help get to the root of and solving the complex objection:

1. Review the problem and the Discovery Agreement to make sure both you and your prospect are addressing the same issue. You may want to check in briefly again with everyone you originally talked to for the Discovery Agreement, whether in person or on the phone, to make sure you haven't veered off course or missed an emerging issue.

2. Ask additional questions to find out what part of the solution doesn't seem to fit the problem. You're likely to hear concerns such as, "That works for my department, but doesn't seem to be a good fit for XYZ department." Checking questions can help you determine what parts of your solution aren't clear, or may not seem a good match.

3. Make appeals that fit the root of the specific objection. The buyer's *task* agenda deals with the technical, practical side of a problem. It usually revolves around two key issues: How to justify the purchase operationally and financially. The personal agenda, on the other hand, concerns *why* a person makes a decision to buy, or the emotional payoffs of a solution – what's in it for him or her.

Your approach should be tailored accordingly. Here are some tactics for appealing to each objection type.

Appealing to the Buyer's Task Agenda

Operational justification for a purchase – how the product or service will increase production, reduce defects, save time, or the like – usually responds to three basic questions:

- Will it work with a minimum of disruption to current operations?
- Is it best among all options for the prospect's situation?
- Will it continue to be best in the future?

Financial justification deals with value, cost effectiveness, and affordability. It responds to such questions as:

- Will it help save or earn money?
- Is it worth the price?
- How will we be able to pay for it?

To deal with these objections, choose one or more of the following tactics. Depending on the particular prospect or situation, one may be more appropriate than others:

It will pay for itself. This method shows how the economic benefits of the product or service will, over time, outweigh the initial purchase price. It demonstrates how the money saved from the use of your offering will pay for that item after a certain period of time. In simple terms, if a company earns or saves a third of its initial investment per year, the machine can be justified as paying for itself in three years. That's not considering benefits the machine generates in year four and beyond.

Return on investment. Here you ask a prospect to think of a purchase as an investment. You show how the client's investment will bring an attractive return either in profits or savings. You arrive at the rate of return by dividing the total money earned or saved by the purchase price. For example, the company that, after five years, has earned or saved $100,000 from the purchase of a $50,000 machine has received a 200 percent return on its investment by the end of the fifth year. A salesperson might say, for example: "Based on these figures, every dollar you invest in this system will return you $4 a year in either savings or additional earnings."

Price vs. cost. Many salespeople dread the moment when they have to reveal the cost of their product. Not because they believe their products are overpriced – knowing their products as they do, they usually believe their price is fair. Rather, they fear *prospects* won't understand the price is fair, no matter how much explaining they do.

If you are more expensive than the competition, there should be valid reasons. Maybe your equipment costs more to make because you use a higher quality of component parts or more money was invested in developing a better design. Or maybe you offer a better, more inclusive warranty. Or you support a broader service network or offer the customer free training in use of your product. If your product costs more, it's up to you to show that as a "total value" it's a better choice than the competition.

Some salespeople do this casually (but with substantial dramatic effect) right in front of the prospect's eyes. They do it by adding up on a sheet of paper, or on a computer screen, all the costs for both competing products. They demonstrate how when the prospect figures in the higher operating, technical support and maintenance costs, lower resale value, etc. of the cheaper product, the total cost of the lower priced competitor may actually be higher. In the meantime, they point out, the prospect will probably enjoy better performance from the more expensive product, too.

You won't sell everybody this way. Some buyers are in a situation where low initial price is vital to their interests at a given point in time. You won't make much headway in that case. But it's amazing how many buyers, once they fully understand all the "shadow" costs in a competitor's product, are willing to pay more up front to get quality.

Cost per unit. This method of justifying price depends on showing how an apparently high initial price is really very reasonable when divided by the number of parts that compose the product.

A variation on this method, called *component cost comparison,* simply reverses this procedure. It consists of assigning a reasonable value to each component of a package. Then the cost of all the components is totaled. When you show that the actual price of the whole package is much lower than the total cost of all the individual components, the prospect can visualize greater value being received for what otherwise might have seemed too high a price.

For example, most stockbrokers charge a fee on every stock trade a client makes. Let's say one company's fee is one percent of the stock's purchase price. Your company, however, offers a customer loyalty program where the customer can make unlimited trades for $10,000 a year plus 0.25 percent of the trades after $1 million. Sounds a bit complicated, so you break it out for the client in the following chart:

Commissions

Trade $	My Company	Competitor
$500,000	$10,000	$5,000
$1 Million	$10,000	$10,000
$2 Million	$12,500	$20,000

Thus, at $2 million in trades, your cost per trade is 0.625% while your competitor's costs is 1.0%. Clearly, if the customer makes $1 million in trades or more, he or she saves money with you.

The personal computer industry has turned this strategy into an art. Sure, you can still buy your computer, software, and peripherals separately, but the industry likes to bundle them together because it can pay far less than the retail price for the same items. The result is that you can buy a complete "plug and go" computer system for considerably less than if you bought the pieces separately. And the good news is that, in most cases, it's a true offer. You would have to pay the full retail price for those same items, so the value to you is quite real.

Appealing to the Personal Motives

People don't really buy our products. Instead, they buy what they imagine those products will *do for them*. No buyers, not even the most jaded corporate purchasing agents, ever buy anything without thinking of the impact it may have on them *personally*.

Sometimes prospects present task objections when what they're really wrestling with is a personal agenda. As a result, it's important to include appeals to the personal agenda in any sales solution, whether it's responding to a specific objection or presenting to an objection-less group. If you've done a good job in the Discovery process, you already should have a handle on decision-makers' personal motives. Here are some ideas for adapting your Advocating approach to the major personal motives:

Appeals to the power motive. The power-oriented buyer is looking for ways to gain greater control over some real, practical aspect of his or her situation. We're not necessarily referring to power in grandiose, cosmic terms. The need for power could show up in something as ordinary as the manager of a parts department wanting to carry a larger inventory of seldom-used parts. If he can do that, he will save himself a lot of headaches – and perhaps look good in other people's eyes as well. He'd like the power to be able to control the situation. If you can suggest how your solution can give that to him, he'll be more likely to buy.

To appeal to the power motive, look for ways to:

1. Increase control of people, procedures, time, or information
2. Increase effectiveness
3. Improve decision-making
4. Choose from options
5. Increase freedom to act
6. Increase authority
7. Increase access to important posts or people
8. Make immediate action possible

Appeals to the recognition motive. For some buyers, the desire for recognition will be the dominant buying motive. Knowing this, the appeals in your presentation should focus on creating favorable visibility for the prospect.

Let's say you work for a company that manufactures computer components. You're calling on the buyer for a large computer manufacturer. You feel this person is recognition oriented and seems to be looking for an opportunity to draw attention to herself through her purchasing and marketing acumen. You have a new item that has been extremely successful in test markets. You might approach her on the basis that this is a) a unique and unusual item, b) that she has a chance to be the first in the market with it, c) that this will put her in a leadership position and d) that Buyer X in another market got a pat on the back for having introduced it in his area.

To appeal to the recognition motive, help the customer:

1. Be a hero or leader
2. Be first
3. Create uniqueness/originality
4. Gain more visibility, chance for publicity
5. Be a change agent – get a chance to make it big
6. Set an example for others
7. Increase talent
8. Be a recognized teacher
9. Enhance self-esteem

Appeals to the approval motive. Approval-oriented buyers want to be sure that others affected by their purchase decision will be pleased. They don't want to rock the boat or ruffle anyone's feathers. One way to appeal to this type of buyer is to show that your product has proved popular with a wide range of people within specific companies that bought it. Another is to provide evidence of your product's popularity in the marketplace in general.

You might also demonstrate how you and your company are willing to share the buying risk by supporting this buyer with a guarantee. As a corollary to sharing the risk, you might also mention others in the buyer's company who favor or support the decision to buy your product (making sure you've confirmed their level of support first, of course.) To appeal to the approval motive, look for ways to:

1. Show it is a popular idea – everybody is doing it
2. Provide after-sale support
3. Assist in selling to others
4. Avoid conflict or controversy
5. Minimize and share the risk
6. Provide supporting data
7. Demonstrate reliability
8. Protect reputations
9. Enhance self-esteem

Appeals to the respect motive. Respect-oriented buyers are motivated by the desire to show and prove their expertise. Being known as the person who knows how things work or why things happen is a source of pride. They're interested in anything that furthers that image.

One appeal that works with this buyer is to show how your product naturally complements the work they've already done, thus reinforcing their own expertise. "Newness" also is an effective appeal because it gives this buyer a chance to build a new domain of knowledge about which he or she will know the most within the company.

Yet another appeal plays off this buyer's need to be right. You can do this by showing how your product substantiates research already done, serves as justification for previous purchases, or reinforces conclusions already made. To appeal to the respect motive, look for ways to:

1. Help the customer be recognized as an expert
2. Share solid research data
3. Provide systematic plans
4. Conduct progress reviews
5. Use written proposals
6. Provide a new talent or skill
7. Use a scientific approach
8. Provide special or unique information
9. Let the customer "do it himself"

The Counselor Approach in Action at IBM

Pat Carey rose to the top of his field selling large-scale IBM computer systems to multinational companies not by being an old-school persuader or features expert, but through his practiced skills as a problem-solver and amateur psychologist. "I see myself as a negotiator," says Carey. "I'm always looking to find the middle ground. I look at what the customer is trying to achieve and how we can help him get there. It's a very straightforward, win-win approach."

Carey taps his background in anthropology, creative writing, and other "front wheel" skill areas more so than technical acumen to make many of his sales. "People think I'm a computer geek, but I really don't know that much about the inner workings of computers," he says. "What I really enjoy is creative problem-solving and deciphering how a person thinks."

When it comes to negotiating price, delivery options, or other sale conditions, for example, Carey has no patience for the salesperson who over-promises and under-delivers. "If it's impossible, I tell customers it's impossible," he says. "I tell them that I will dissatisfy them by trying to satisfy them, and they usually appreciate that honesty. Weak salespeople will promise what they can't deliver just to get out of the room, but it's like children's lies – they keep building until you have a much bigger problem."

Carey also doesn't look at a key step in the selling process, closing the sale, in the same do-or-die terms many salespeople are taught to see it. "Closing is more of a natural extension of work you've already done," he says. "Sure, the buyer has to sign a formal document, but it seems very minor after you've gone through all the work to get there. I don't even think about closing the sale because the client and I work together so closely that it becomes more of a mutual agreement than a 'sale' in the traditional sense."

Carey also points to customer service, and the ability to honor customers' perceptions of a given situation – not necessarily whether they are right or wrong – as another key to sales success. "Customer satisfaction is an unnatural act. We don't like to admit we're wrong or that everything isn't perfect, and that's what we often have to do," he says. "As a result, I think of it not as a question of what the customer is asking for, but why this particular customer needs special attention."

He gives an example. Early in his career he was managing a grocery store, and had an elderly customer who came in nearly every day to complain about something. "The staff hated her, but I figured she was just a lonely person, desperate for some human contact," Carey says. "One day she came in while I was working the customer service counter. She said the cabbage she had just purchased was bad. I got a very serious look on my face, took the cabbage from her and examined it closely. Then I gave it a whack with my hand and said, 'Bad cabbage, bad, bad cabbage.' I handed it back to her and said, 'I think it'll be better now.'" The customer-from-hell laughed for the first time anyone could remember and, from then, on sought Carey out for short conversations. Yes, she was a challenging customer, but one who regularly spent money in the store and only required a bit of special attention.

5 | Supporting Skills

We've all experienced the feeling. We're excited about the new computer system, new office space, or new car we've just agreed to purchase, but as the transfer of money approaches, the adrenaline rush disappears, and our throats clench up. "Have I made a mistake?" we ask. "I can't afford this. The company doesn't need this. It can't be as durable as advertised. I'm in trouble."

It's called buyer's remorse and happens in many sales settings, from the purchase of a simple piece of clothing to a multimillion-dollar piece of manufacturing equipment. The bigger the buying decision, the more money involved, the more people affected, the more likely such second-guessing will occur. A whole new chapter in the sales process begins once you actually close the sale. You may have performed the Relating, Discovering, and Advocating processes extremely well, but the nagging doubt that creeps in when the client actually commits money to something can erase all of your hard work.

We don't always see buyer's remorse. Often it's cloaked in stalling or diversionary behavior, rather than direct verbal complaint. Buyers rarely come right out and say, "I'm afraid." Instead, they let out their tension in the form of defensive behavior, often directed at you.

THE "NO HURRY" PHENOMENON

The Supporting step actually begins before a contract is signed or a check is cut. It happens right after you've made your recommendation in the Advocating step. The customer may agree that it's a good decision, yet something is holding him back or creating anxiety. An imminent case of buyer's remorse often reveals itself in comments or behaviors like these:

- "It's kind of risky to make this purchase with the economy so uncertain."
- "There's really no hurry."
- "I still have to run this by a few more people."
- "The rumor is that we're getting a new VP of purchasing, so I can't go forward quite yet."
- Failure to return your phone calls.
- Changing the subject.
- Postponing meetings repeatedly.

In fact, these "reasons" often have little to do with the purchase decision. What's really going on is that the customer is nervous, and the anxiety manifests in these stalling tactics. Prospects on the defensive use two behaviors to reduce their tension: fight or flight. They can attack the salesperson, the company, or the product – that's the fight. Or they can stall for time, make excuses, or raise vague objections that can't be pinned down. They leave you guessing about what's happening – the flight. Flight behavior almost always contains some version of "Don't call me. I'll call you." Prospects may even show both flight and fight behaviors in the same selling situation.

Buyers adopt these "no hurry" attitudes and behaviors any time they're not sure that the reward of their buying decisions will far outweigh any possible penalties or punishments. Those fears are usually tied to the *task* or *personal* motives we've explored in earlier chapters.

Some common task fears are:

Loss of profit. "Will this new computer system create new efficiencies – or be a financial drain? I could be taking it on the chin with this one."

Excessive cost. "I'm going to have to cut back in other areas to pay for this. But what other areas?"

Poor performance. "Sure they say it's reliable. But what if it doesn't measure up to the kind of job we want it to do? Or what if it turns out to be a lemon?"

Increased effort. "Contracting with this new vendor means just one thing as far as I'm concerned. More work."

Customers also might feel a personal fear such as:

Loss of power. "If I buy this new software, the one who is really going to be the big winner is Shirley. She's the one they will go to for solutions instead of me."

Loss of recognition. "I've made some good, sound decisions for this company in the past. They expect it from me. What if this one turns out to be a mistake?"

Disapproval. "I can just hear them upstairs if this one doesn't fly. My job could be on the line."

Loss of respect. "The problem is if this doesn't work, I'll be the laughing stock of the whole division."

Until you can resolve these concerns in the minds of prospects and support them in making sound rational and emotional decisions, there's little hope they'll be in any hurry to make a commitment to you.

THE ZONE OF INDIFFERENCE

Whether a formal purchase contract has been signed or not, you and your customer have entered the "Zone of Indifference." It's so named because customers in this transitory period don't yet have strong feelings either of satisfaction or dissatisfaction. Most in the zone feel a lit-

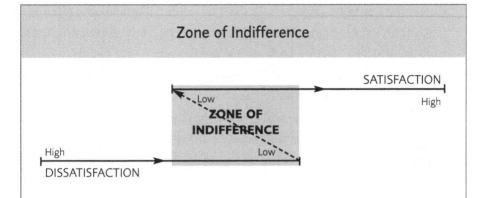

Zone of Indifference

SATISFACTION

Low

High

ZONE OF
INDIFFERENCE

High

Low

DISSATISFACTION

Satisfaction and dissatisfaction are not opposites – they are two separate conditions. Buyers can experience varying degrees of each. When buyers experience low levels of satisfaction, they may also experience low levels of dissatisfaction. This middle area is called the Zone of Indifference, because buyers do not have strong feelings of satisfaction or dissatisfaction.

tle unsettled and are waiting to determine if they're happy or not. If they have signed a contract, they may feel regret or even some panic. If they haven't signed, many find excuses for putting off the purchase decision.

Although their rhetoric or body language may indicate otherwise, customers in the zone probably aren't *dissatisfied.* They just need some emotional support and reassurance. "Customers are easily pushed in one direction or another when they're in this zone," says Keith Sondrall, a Wilson Learning facilitator. "If you make a mistake in this period, such as ignoring them or taking them for granted, they will quickly become dissatisfied customers. If you expertly support their buying decision, they will become satisfied."

And it's well documented how valuable a "very satisfied" customer can be to your business. For one thing, it's easier to sell more product to an existing customer than attract a new one. Research from the National Sales Council in Washington, D.C. shows that it's about three times more expensive to land a new customer than expand relationships with existing ones. That is because of the high advertising, promotion, and prospecting costs necessary to secure new clients.

Delighted customers also are quick to talk you up to their friends, professional associates, family members, or any others they can corner for a conversation. They will recommend you to other department heads in their companies and reorder from you with few questions. That kind of word of mouth is especially powerful in today's networked global community. Good sales or service experiences – as well as the nightmare variety – can spread like wildfire via e-mail, chat rooms, and newsgroups. In addition, research from the customer service consulting firm, e-satisfy.com (formerly the Technical Assistance Research Programs or TARP), shows that customers who have had a problem or concern effectively resolved can be even *more* loyal to your company than had they never had a problem at all.

HELPING VS. CONTROLLING:
THE FOUR PILLARS OF SUPPORT

Any good Supporting mechanism is solid and multi-faceted. Build a house on top of two footings and you can have more than a few problems. But stabilize it with four moorings and you have a structure that can withstand a great deal of adversity.

So it is with Supporting our customers in this last stage of the selling process. By using the four Supporting pillars recommended here, you'll meet all of your customer's needs in that uncertain time between making a buy decision and product or service implementation. And you'll create a foundation for an ongoing, long-term relationship, as well.

The four pillars are: 1) Supporting the Buying Decision 2) Managing Implementation 3) Dealing with Dissatisfaction and 4) Enhancing the Relationship. These four strategies will answer the questions that weigh most heavily on the customer's mind in the post-sale environment:

- How do I know that, in my case, you'll turn out to be what you say you are?
- How do I know that, in my case, your solution will perform the way you say it will?
- How do I really know your solution is the best one?
- How do I know your solution will continue to be the best down the road, given the rapid pace of change in the market?

The First Pillar: Supporting the Buying Decision

Tevilla Riddell, principal of The Riddell Resources Group in Cincinnati and a senior consultant with Wilson Learning, remembers the day she bought her new Saab. "I was excited about the car, but it suddenly hit me that I'd made a big investment and I wasn't sure if I could afford it," Riddell says. Luckily, her Saab salesperson was adept at Supporting her buying decision. A short follow-up phone call made a big impact. "He called, and I mentioned my remorse," Riddell says. "He could have ignored me after the sale but instead reminded me that this was a good investment, stressed how a Saab holds its value and would be easy to resell in the future if needed, so I wouldn't lose money. I'm not sure how I would have felt had he not called, but I do know that I wouldn't have felt as good about the purchase as quickly as I did."

That's the purpose behind the first pillar of Supporting: to keep the customer feeling good about the purchase. You will mitigate remorse or second thoughts and increase the odds of building a long-term relationship with the customer or getting valuable referrals. "If you don't support the buying decision at this stage, and the person has buyer's remorse, you can have problems down the line," says Don Luce, managing director of ELA Sales, a consulting group and authorized representative of Wilson Learning in San Francisco. "That doubt will extend into the next purchase decision."

Here are some things you can do to reduce buyer anxiety in the post-sale environment:

- **Call.** Call your contacts a few days after you close a sale. Thank them for their business and ask if you can answer additional questions. Sure, making these calls takes some time away from prospecting or other sales duties, but it has big payoff in terms of customer loyalty and word of mouth. The key here is to follow up as often as the customer wants, no more, no less. You want to show you care but you don't want to be a pest. On the day you close the sale, ask how often the person would like to talk to you.

- **Congratulate buyers on the purchase.** Send a card or just give them a hearty handshake. Reaffirm that they made the right choice.

- **Add a benefit.** Save a small product benefit that may not have been worth mentioning in the Advocating stage and highlight it now. Car salespeople might say, "Oh, I forgot to mention that there's a promotion going on, and this car comes with a free upgrade to a CD player." These "after the fact" benefits aren't costly to you or your company, but they can keep customers focused on something positive and reinforce their belief that they made the perfect buying decision.

- **Don't overreact to fear.** "When customers say they are wondering if they made the right decision, the tendency for salespeople is to spew out everything they've already told them about this being the right product or service for their needs," says Luce. "Instead, step back and listen to what customers are really saying. If they're concerned about the price tag, remind them of the savings to the bottom line in the end, but don't panic and pull out every feature and benefit you can remember from your arsenal. You've already done that. You just need to hold their hands a bit here."

- **Reassure in the style they prefer.** There's no one-size-fits-all formula for handling customers' anxieties at this stage. Revisit your assessment of their behavioral or "social style," and determine what tactics will work best to reassure them that they made a good decision.

Among the tactics you might choose from:

1. Send case studies featuring other companies that have had sustained success implementing your product or service. Whereas in Advocating you might have used the experience of only one satisfied customer, now is the time to tell about quantities of satisfied users. This way it's no longer your opinion, but the opinion of third parties with no ax to grind. The key to reassurance in this stage is believability.

2. Send research reports – from independent sources, if possible – on how your product performed in field trials.

3. Send articles from industry trade magazines or other publications that highlight how your product's been used successfully in the field.

4. Offer to talk to other decision makers or purchase influencers in the customer's company about the product.

5. If convenient, bring the customer or other decision makers to your home office to meet top managers or people in charge of product support.

6. Type up a formal version of the product's pros and cons for them.

7. Offer a free trial period. This works well with products that are easily transportable, such as computer software.

8. Emphasize the warranty. A strong warranty can help persuade fence sitters. Who doesn't sleep easier after buying a car with a 5-year warranty? Since companies don't want to lose their shirts on such warranties, the agreements offer reassurance that the product is reliable and mechanically sound.

9. Stay in the Counselor mindset. There is always the chance that this suddenly is not the right decision for the customer. That can happen, and when it does, it's important to remember your role is to counsel them, not to make this one sale. By explaining options in changing the contract or modifying the purchase rather than pressuring, you will build greater trust and often more than recoup any losses from this one sale down the road.

The Second Pillar: Managing the Implementation

Product or service implementation can be an anxious time for sales-people because it signals the point where they hand off customers to someone else, relinquishing a level of control over customer satisfaction. Suddenly you're not in charge anymore. Some customers resent it when they're suddenly handed off to new people, as though you pulled some kind of "bait and switch" on them. Other customers will work to keep you involved more than you should be, calling you for questions that really should go to the installation team. Either way, you can get caught in the middle.

To make an implementation transition more seamless, use these tactics:

- Make a list of everyone involved in the implementation process – both on your team and the customers' – that includes their responsibilities, phone numbers, and e-mail addresses.
- Create a list of the exact steps that will occur in implementation, an estimate of how long each will take, how the client will know when each step is completed, and who the primary contact for the customer will be at each stage should there be questions or problems.
- Personally introduce key people on your installation team to key people on your customer's team.
- Keep your ear to the ground. Don't meddle with the implementation, but stay in touch with the team to make sure everything is going smoothly. Offer to help if there are concerns. Occasionally, you will be able to provide valuable information to the implementation team on the company's culture, the role (and quirks) of certain personalities, and so on.
- Manage details behind the scenes. A good residential real estate agent, for example, will handle much of the legwork with a loan company, the closing firm, and other involved parties to take some pressure off their client, the homebuyer. It's a time eater, but it often

keeps first-time homebuyers who can easily become overwhelmed with the process from dropping out. It's the little things you do behind the scenes that keep the gears running smoothly and often lead to repeat business and referrals.

- Generate reports. If the installation is complex or has multiple phases, provide a weekly update to customers of what's been completed, progress compared to schedule and, other related issues. It'll help everyone rest a bit easier.

The Third Pillar: Proactively Handling Dissatisfaction

Sometimes there are real problems after a sale is completed. Many times, those problems are beyond the control of your customer. Perhaps her company was recently purchased, a new purchasing manager was hired, or a new company president with a new corporate strategy was appointed. Maybe the customer's next-year budget was just slashed or priorities were reordered as a result of an unexpected quarterly report.

Other times, the dissatisfaction originates from actions taken by the salesperson's company. "We find that in most cases when a customer moves from the zone of indifference to being dissatisfied, it's because of a policy at the company they are purchasing from," says Luce. "It's rarely the fault only of the salesperson. It could be the delivery staff being unwilling to change its schedule or the accounts billable people demanding extra paperwork, for example."

Whether the problems are created by the client's company or your own, the last thing you want to do is play the blame game. Here are some tactics for resolving the situation without pointing fingers.

Reintroduce the LSCPA Process. The key is to get to the heart of the real problem, which is sometimes camouflaged by the customer's defensive or diversionary behavior. The customer might be saying the product implementation is taking too long when, in fact, the real problem is that he's getting pressure from above to justify the purchase decision. Here's where a return to the LSPCA regimen from Chapter 3 can help. To reiterate the process:

Listen to the customer. Let him or her vent. Don't judge what's being said. Encourage the flow of feelings and let the tension out.

Share your understanding of the customer's situation. Play back to the customer what he or she has said to show you've heard or understood. Sharing doesn't mean agreeing, only indicating that you grasp the customer's perception of the situation.

Clarify that the concern the customer has expressed is the real objection. Restate the customer's words so the real problem becomes apparent – and becomes a question that can be answered.

Problem Solve by discussing potential solutions that address the customer's real concern.

Ask for Action by recommending a solution or next step, and ask for the customer's agreement.

A customer's problem is your problem, even at this stage. Too often salespeople bow out of the process when an implementation team takes over. When things aren't going well, though, the first person that customer will call is the person who sold them the product because he or she has built up the rapport. It's very easy to say, "I don't handle that any more," or "It's the installation team's problem." But you need to remember that this is still your customer, even at this stage. And that means staying engaged until acceptable solutions are found to your customer's concerns.

Resolving Common Post-Sale Complaints

Even if something goes wrong for the customer following a sale, you can cement customer loyalty and gain powerful word-of-mouth advertising if you use effective recovery strategies. Here are a few field-tested tactics for dealing with common post-sale problems:

1. **The Price Has Gone Up.** You sell a petroleum-based product and the price of petroleum just skyrocketed. Your customer contracted for a year's worth of product delivered monthly, and now, a few months later, you have to tell her the price jumped dramatically. What do you do?

   - Be straightforward and honest. Tell her exactly what factors made the price increase necessary.
   - Give her plenty of notice. Never spring a price increase on anyone without allowing for time to adjust budgets or prices to your client's customers.
   - Show your concern. If this is a large price increase, listen, and let the customer vent without interrupting. However, in the end, gently remind her that you can't control factors such as the price of petroleum.
   - Look for creative solutions. Perhaps the customer can buy a larger quantity of product at a time and get a bigger volume discount. Or maybe she can substitute a slightly different, less expensive product from your product line in 10 percent of the cases. The key is to get creative in seeking solutions.

2. **It Doesn't Work Right.** The equipment is installed and should be up and running. But the line keeps going down because one of your products is malfunctioning. What do you do?

   - If you can't diagnose the trouble through phone calls, send a fix-it team out immediately to determine if it's a parts or mechanical problem, a user problem, or a problem with the match between the technology and its job.
   - If it's a user problem, consider offering free, one-time training to all the machine's core users.
   - If it's a parts problem, fix it free of charge and work to compensate the company for any lost production time. You might offer,

a future discount on supplies, for example.

- If the problem is a poor match between the machine and required tasks, circle back through the Discovering and Advocating steps to make sure you made the right recommendation. There is always the chance something changed after the purchase was finalized.

3. **Promised Value Doesn't Materialize.** You sold a new computer system to a large multinational corporation, and user support is costing them US$10,000 a year. You and your team arrived at this figure by assessing the usage and support patterns of a similar client. The problem is, this particular client isn't using the service much and now thinks the price is unreasonable. What do you do?

- Conduct a needs survey to determine if there are areas where the client could be using the service more – pockets of the company where the service might significantly increase productivity and proficiency or limit downtime.
- Revise the contract, if necessary, to reflect fewer hours of use. But keep monitoring the situation to make sure it doesn't change.
- Suggest alternatives for providing additional value, such as offering free training to employees or free training on upgrades to all users, or suggest giving the client access to other business expertise in your company.

4. **That's Not Covered.** Your customer drives in with steam billowing out of the radiator of his car. You discover there's a leak, and the vehicle is less than one month past warranty. The customer thinks you should cover it because the leak most likely started before the warranty expired but was too small to notice. Your service department says no way. What do you do?

- Don't walk away. Sure, you're in sales and not service, but if you imply that it's not your problem, the likelihood of ever seeing that customer again – or getting any referrals from him – drops to zero. And the odds on bad press rise exponentially.

- Determine if the customer has a valid claim. Do a little research on your own, and find out the likelihood of the leak starting while the car was still under warranty. Perhaps you can convince the service manager that a warranty shouldn't expire just because a customer is too busy to notice a small problem. Perhaps you can convince him that in "tough call" cases like this, the long-term benefit in customer satisfaction outweighs the short-term cost of repair.

- Work to find other solutions. If your hands truly are tied, be upfront with the customer. But offer something – a free loaner vehicle while the car is being repaired or some other form of atonement – to soften the blow and let him know you care.

- Be proactive. While it will not help this customer, learn from this experience. Maybe you can call or send a message to current customers whose warranties will expire in a month, offering an inspection to avoid a necessary repair like this.

The Fourth Pillar: Enhancing the Relationship

You've made the sale. The implementation went off without a hitch, and the customer reports he's as happy as a clam. You could pull up stakes and move on to the next prospect. Or you could maximize the work you did in Relating, Discovering, and Advocating steps and look for more business from this customer or his company. This is the time to get deeper into the company and find out what else you can offer. You've built a strong relationship that can carry you a long way.

Think about it. Salespeople can make their sales grow in two ways: by adding new accounts on their own through hit-and-miss prospecting or through account penetration – securing more business within existing accounts or leveraging them for expansion.

Here are some ways to enhance and broaden your relationship with customers following a sale:

- Go to the top. Assuming that your product or service makes a positive impact in the company, ask your satisfied customer to help you get a meeting with top management. The goal is to gain a broader picture of the business and determine where your products or services might be a good fit in other areas of the company.
- Ask to interview managers or employees using the product. One goal is to find out how the product is working for them, what improvements might be made, and how you might add value. As a result, you may discover needs in other areas that your organization could fill and identify managers who might offer testimonials for your product. In essence, you're starting the Discovery process all over.
- Look for other opportunities to create value in the customer's company. You don't want customers to view your attempts to add value simply as excuses for raising prices or tacking on costly little extras. Timing and sincerity are crucial to adding value at this stage. If you think of it as a tool for manipulating customers, if you keep track of your favors, or if you only do it when it's advantageous for you to be in the other person's good graces, you'll lose credibility. So use this approach with integrity.

If there's ever an ideal time to do something that establishes you as a friend or helper, it's after the sale. That's when it's least likely to be regarded as a conditional expression of friendship and more likely to be accepted as a true-blue act of caring.

A few ideas:

- Pass on a business-related idea, not necessarily about your own product, but perhaps other products that may be of help to the client.

Servicing the Sale
The Four Pillars of Supporting

Supporting Foundations	Salesperson Activities
Support the Buying Decision	• Reduce customer anxiety • Make follow-up call (phone and face-to-face) • Ask for feedback • Provide value-added service
Manage the Implementation	• Keep in touch to minimize post-sale anxiety • Assist with the approval process • Introduce support resources • Monitor and report progress • Determine how and when to stay in touch after implementation
Deal with Dissatisfaction	• Empathize with the customer's feelings • Respond to problems with LSCPA • Continue to anticipate customer concerns and expectations • Reinforce the benefits
Enhance the Relationship	• Be available • Arrange for continued personal communication • Facilitate open, candid, organizational communication • Add value • Maintain the quality of the products/services provided • Provide ongoing updates and progress reports • Become a resource for information, help, ideas and problem solving • Grow the business internally • Ask the customer for names of qualified referrals • Establish interdependent networks between your organization and the customer's company

- Share non-business advice on everything from day care to car repair to vacation experiences.
- Send along a book or magazine article you think might be useful.
- Recommend allied or associated products or services when your own company can't fill a customer request.
- Offer free training on your products and services to end-users. The exposure can have particular value if those users are distributors.
- Offer to co-sponsor an open house and information-sharing session for your client companies' customers.
- Strive to build an interdependent relationship between your firm and the customer's company. You want the customer to view your company as an entire organization – not just one salesperson – dedicated to his or her success and to understanding the challenges in his or her business. To that end, you might encourage your company's accountants to share theories of accountancy with a start-up company, or you might ask your marketing experts to spare some time to talk about tactics for penetrating new markets. If your client is considering expanding globally, someone on your staff might provide pointers on the logistics of shipping product overseas, including dealing with customs requirements. Look to establish these types of connections and relationships whenever possible.

Indeed, smart salespeople know that adding value isn't simply about the extras but about the experience and knowledge they can lend to clients' companies to help them operate more efficiently or effectively. It's the kind of expertise that might cost clients a lot of money to develop or hire on their own – but costs you very little to provide.

ADDING VALUE THROUGH EXPERTISE AND NETWORKING

Here are some examples of salespeople who expanded existing relationships with clients, or laid the groundwork for capturing future business, by using the Counselor salesperson's Supporting strategy:

- John Thompson sells computerized cash registers for National Cash Register in New York City. His contact at a new account, a large toy manufacturer, mentioned offhandedly that his company was working to create an Internet-based purchasing system. "That prompted to me to ask if I could talk to top management to see if there was anything we could do to help," Thompson says. "I discovered that their plan was to do about 50 percent of their purchasing over the Internet within the next five years. We had just acquired a small company that develops software for secure Internet purchases. It proved to be a great fit for them."

- As a salesman for Goodyear Corporation in Des Moines, Iowa, Bill Williams sells tires for industrial equipment and semi-truck fleets. During a meeting with the CEO of a client trucking company, the CEO mentioned that his company was trying to use its fleet more efficiently. "I had read in our company newsletter that our own fleet manager had instituted a rigorous backhauling program that required the hiring of just one employee but had made the company a lot of money in one year," Williams says. "I got the two fleet managers in touch to discuss the program and ended up looking like something of a hero. It was really no big deal for me. I just did some natural networking."

- Fred St. George sells timing devices for use on military equipment and weaponry for Multime Company in St. Louis. When visiting with a client one day, he noticed that several people in the office were using new laptop computers. "My brother-in-law owns a small computer training company, and I mentioned that if they needed any training, he'd probably be pretty good," St. George says. "It turns out they were looking for some affordable, customized training for their sales staff to make sure they got the most out of the new computers, and the contact paid off for them."

Counselor Selling
in Action

From your early years, people have warned that the real world can be unpredictable and a little frightening. Only hard-won experience, they counseled, could provide answers to life's most vexing questions. And as a professional salesperson you know the truth of that view. The real sales world can be volatile, uncivil, and at times unforgiving. It pays to remember that "learning experiences" are often costly but necessary steps toward performance with fulfillment.

This chapter is designed to help you navigate the whitewater you'll invariably encounter as you start to use Counselor-selling strategies in the field. Despite your best efforts, at times you'll face prospects who'll take left turns when you fully expect a right and who will fill your work days with more frustration than fulfillment.

The best Counselor sellers know how to extract positive results from the most challenging or seemingly futile circumstances. To give you some real life lessons, we've chronicled some of the most common obstacles faced by salespeople today. These are challenges that cut across industries, product or service types, and selling modes. In each case, you'll see how Counselor-based solutions were applied.

We hope they help light the way for your own sales journey.

YOUR CLIENT IS JUST COMPARING PRICES
Situation:
Your prospect has already made up his mind to go with a competitor and is simply building a case for his negotiations with that seller.

Solution:
They key is to identify this as a problem before you put too much time into the sale. If you've built a good rapport with the right people before you're called in for a proposal, you should be able to pick up on clues sent early in the sales process. Listen for phrases such as:

Group One:
- How do your product's features compare with those of your competition?
- What's your best price?
- What are your delivery and payment terms?

Group Two:
- We've already met with ABC Company, and their product offers a sound solution. What are your impressions of that product?
- We're really just comparison-shopping at this point.
- We don't want any custom options. Just give us your best "off the rack" solution.

The first group of phrases indicates a decision already has been made. Why would decision makers be focused on price or delivery terms, for example, if their foremost concern were how your product could solve a pressing business problem? Such questions beyond the Relating stage of a sales process suggest prospects are looking for information to justify their case or to satisfy an internal purchasing policy requiring a certain number of proposals.

The second group of phrases indicates that quality – purchasing the absolute best product for a need – isn't the prospect's top concern. In fact, some of the queries suggest a lack of seriousness about buying product at all. In all likelihood, a decision already was sealed before you arrived.

These clues should emerge fairly quickly if you regularly practice the Purpose/Process/Payoff approach introduced in Chapter 1. When you start with purpose – "Why we are meeting?" – the customer probably will cut you short and come in with his own reason. If you don't get the hint here that the prospect isn't serious, you should early in the Discovery stage. Prospects will be reluctant to answer some of your fact-finding and feeling-finding questions and may not grant you permission to ask in-depth questions about their business or buying needs.

Don't fret if this happens to you on a new account. Look at the time you take to build rapport not as a waste, but as laying the groundwork for future opportunities with that prospect. If you're the first one to educate the prospect about your product category, odds are you'll also be the first one called when it comes time for a purchase decision. As tough as it may be, it's important to sympathize with the customer's situation. By putting together a quick, no-frills proposal, you'll help him meet his needs – and limit your own time investment.

If you have a good relationship with the prospect, be honest with him. Let him know your assessment of the situation and tell him that you'll be happy to put together some numbers for him. However, make it clear that next time you'll both be better served with more honesty up front, allowing both sides to save time and energy.

If you find yourself in this situation with an existing account, things may be more dire. Most ethical clients won't bring you in to help pad the purchasing process. Certainly you'll have some long-tenured clients who make a decision without asking your advice, but they should respect you enough as a professional Counselor not to ask you to do busy work.

If this situation does happen with an existing client, first ask yourself these questions:

- Have any of the key decision makers in the company recently changed?
- Has my credibility (or my company's credibility) eroded for some reason in the mind of the client?

- Has the client company's culture or purchasing philosophy changed as a result of a merger, new management, or other activity? If so, consider revisiting propriety or even competence issues from the Relating stage of the Counselor process.
- Have I used Purpose/Process/Payoff in every meeting?

Odds are that something has changed in your relationship with the client or in their perception of you or your offerings. You need a new strategy. It's a good idea to ask yourself these questions throughout any sales process, regardless of your suspicions about client intentions, to help prevent these situations before they end up costing you valuable time or sales.

YOUR CLIENT TAKES THE JOB INSIDE

Situation:
After weeks of working with a new prospect to discover his needs and craft the perfect solution, you are ready to advocate your solution formally. However, the client calls and tells you he's decided to handle the solution internally after you supplied mountains of painstaking analysis.

Solution:
Welcome to the unforgiving world of sales. The reality is most of your hard work is fair game if done in the client's name.

While this scenario is more frequent in the consulting and service world, where problem analysis represents a large percentage of a salesperson's time investment, it happens to all salespeople in varying degrees.

If you sell insurance, for example, you can spend days or even weeks determining the right type of coverage for a prospect, and he can turn around and take that research directly to his current carrier or insurance brokerage firm. Or perhaps you sell external marketing services. After you've done the research and determined what type of marketing campaign best fits the prospect's needs, there's little stopping the prospect from simply saying no thanks, then handing his internal marketing department your plan to incorporate into its own.

The best solution, of course, is to figure out as soon as possible that you're being used in this manner. Although nothing's foolproof, these clues in Relating or Discovering stages can help:

- A shaky reputation in your industry. Ask around with your competitors or colleagues in sales associations to see if the prospect has ever done anything like this to them.

- Quota-type inferences. If your contact at the prospect business says, "We're just trying to make sure we aren't missing anything," it may be a red flag.

- Problem analyzed. Waiting for a solution. If the prospect has all of his problems accurately diagnosed and is simply waiting for your review, it could be a signal he's stuck on finding a solution, but has plenty of staff or resources standing ready to implement it once found, without paying for external help.

- Vague decision-making timelines. The prospect says, "We're not sure about the time line on this" or, more ominously, "We still don't know if we'll have the budget for this."

- Signals from purchase influencers. One of the peripheral people you interview during the Discovery stage might say, "I don't understand why they're asking you to do all this work."

- Classified ads. Ads in the newspaper or on the Internet for positions at the prospect company in your area of expertise might indicate the prospect is picking your brain for information but intends to hire someone to provide internally the same services or expertise you offer.

Now What?

If you think your sales relationship is at risk in such a scenario, there are three different steps you might take:

1. **Bow out gracefully.** While you don't want to risk future business with the prospect, you can say that your preliminary analysis indicates the need can be handled internally. If the prospect agrees, offer a few "value added" ideas for solving the problem or building goodwill like, "I know XYZ company used the new Quicken software with good results" or "One client of mine developed a monthly newsletter for customers to help respond to problems like that." It shows your willingness to be a Counselor salesperson but without having to invest any more time in the sale.

2. **Charge for analysis.** One insurance company we know of provides its commercial prospects with an insurance needs analysis valued at $70,000, equivalent to what a leading independent consultant might charge. If the prospect buys the company's insurance, the analysis is free. If they decide not to buy, they pay about half price ($30,000) for the analysis. Such pay structures, increasingly popular today, are a way to ensure up-front time investments and commitment of expertise show some revenue return.

3. **Take the risk.** You could continue to pursue the business with confidence that it's still winnable or to lay the groundwork for future opportunities. If you take this tack, make it worth your while. For instance, will the problem analysis you do be transferable to other clients in this industry? What might you gain from this interaction that could help land business with similar clients? What are the odds the client might use you on future projects? If those odds are good, this might be a great opportunity to demonstrate your expertise, regardless of whether you land the business this go around.

YOUR NON-PROFIT RATES LOOK TOO LOW

Situation:

You work for a non-profit consulting firm. Because you receive government grants, you can offer some services at lower prices than the competition. The problem is that prospects don't believe your offering is as good as your for-profit competitors' because it's so cheap.

Solution:

This is a tough problem that plagues more than non-profit organizations. Any salesperson offering a significant cost advantage over his competition will face the same suspicion about products or services: *just why is your price so much lower?*

Some organizations offer services that accompany or extend beyond their core competency areas, but price these services very competitively – or offer them free as a value added service or *loss leader*. For example, grocery distributors have a great deal of knowledge about how to design grocery stores. When a grocery store signs on as a new account, the distributor often asks if they can provide design advice, usually at low cost or even free. The store's managers naturally would be wary of the quality of this "free advice."

The key here is to move the focus deftly from the price of your product to your expertise and to provide a clear, believable explanation of why your costs are lower. You'll need to spend more time establishing credibility than if your offerings were priced higher. You can do this by:

- Developing a short presentation that explains your organization's mission and why your services are cheaper, backed up with testimonials of past success. The grocery distributor might say that its mission is to build efficient delivery networks. Without successful grocery stores, its business will suffer as well, so it's to the distributor's advantage to provide design advice cheaply or at no cost. A non-profit organization can quickly explain about its government funding and how it can funnel that funding into hiring talented staff that might otherwise be spent on advertising, marketing, high taxes, or other costs if it were a for-profit enterprise.
- Creating a written document outlining your areas of expertise and clients successfully served. Prospects will constantly compare you to other available options. Don't let them wonder what your quali-

fications are. List every applicable achievement.

- Explaining in detail why your costs are lower than the competition's, if you're a for-profit company. Maybe you sell direct or, for example, conduct transactions on the Internet, which allows you to save middlemen costs, or perhaps your overhead is lower. Whatever the rationale, your prospects will need to hear it.
- Focusing on the team. List the qualifications of every team member that might serve the client, including other reputable companies those people have worked for.
- Providing an exact comparison of your services with your top competitors' services. Show that you can offer all the same services in your area of expertise, at a lower cost.
- Showing your human side. The tendency in these situations is to try to drill your product advantages or consulting expertise into the prospect's brain. Avoid overkill, and remember to take a break occasionally to show your human side. Ask the prospect about common friends or associates you might have in the business. Establish your credibility as a nice person, too.

YOU RUN INTO GATEKEEPERS

Situation:

You're having a difficult time getting past gatekeepers to reach true decision makers in a prospect firm. Perhaps you sell to the pharmaceutical industry, for example, and can't get past human-shield receptionists to the physicians who write prescriptions or approve drug purchases.

Solution:

Ah, gatekeepers. Aren't they wonderful? They may be receptionists in their first job after graduation or seasoned administrative assistants instructed to protect the organization's decision makers from salesperson assaults. The problem, of course, is that our products and services have real value to decision makers, but without that critical support from gatekeepers, we'll never get a chance to show them what they're missing.

Above all, as a salesperson you need to show respect for the gatekeeper. He or she would not be in that position if the customer did not see value in that role. Ultimately, you want that gatekeeper to be a support for your sales efforts. Treated well at the beginning of the relationship, the gatekeeper may be able to get you in when you need an emergency meeting with the customer, so your effort to be courteous from the beginning will serve you well at closing time. Here are some tactics that might help you in working with a gatekeeper.

Say you're that pharmaceutical salesperson selling to physicians and health care plan administrators. You can probe the gatekeepers' defenses with these tactics:

- Ask for a very short appointment – just 15 minutes – to share some industry news or information. In today's rapidly evolving business world, all buyers need to stay abreast of new products, and they often welcome such short informational visits. If a customer can't fit you in under such conditions (provided he or she is not being bombarded with requests) he or she probably doesn't want to see salespeople at all. You may then need to seek out other purchasers.
- Ask the gatekeeper if he or she was instructed not to schedule salespeople to visit. If the answer is yes, proceed to other tactics. If the answer is no, have a pithy, provocative description of your product's benefits ready – testimonials tend to work well – to convince the gatekeeper that you deserve one of the coveted time slots.
- If you've met with the customer before, be sure to mention it. That familiarity often is enough to persuade a gatekeeper to let you in.

Extreme Measures

If you're dealing with an extreme case of gatekeeping, you need to try some extreme measures. Here are some tactics that have worked for practicing pharmaceutical salespeople interviewed for this book:

1. **Hold an educational event.** Then make sure to give a valuable, concise-but-compelling presentation about your product, new legislation, or trends. Successful pharmaceutical salespeople have used the "lunch-and-learn" presentation format effectively for years.

2. **Get the customer's e-mail address.** Receptionists or assistants often refer you to e-mail if you truthfully say you have a short message about some new products. Say you don't want to waste your customer's time so you'd rather send e-mail. Once you have the address, you can develop a targeted marketing campaign based on short messages designed to educate the customer. But the last thing you want to do is flood his or her inbox with rambling e-mails. Make sure there's a time lapse between messages and that what you send is short and to the point.

3. **Probe for peripheral needs.** For example, the customer may be expanding his offices. Might you lend your company's chief accountant or legal advisor for an hour to advise on technical concerns? The goal is to build a relationship, so such offerings at this point can help set you apart from the masses.

4. **Use testimonials.** If there are other customers happy with your product, write a short letter or e-mail mentioning this to the prospect. This kind of testimonial might be enough to pique some interest, at least enough to get you into the office for a short visit.

5. **Place articles in industry publications.** Articles in respected trade publications that mention your product will rate highly on the credibility scale. Send these along with product fact sheets to targeted customers, and then follow up with e-mails or phone calls.

YOUR CLIENT'S BUDGET SUDDENLY GETS CUT

Situation:

You have done a good job building rapport with a prospect and discovering his needs. You even have preliminary sign off on the solution you've advocated. But now the client says his budget has been cut, and he can't go with your recommendation.

Solution:

We wish this were a rare occurrence for salespeople, but in tough economic times it can be the norm rather than the exception. Such a revelation can be demoralizing, especially if you've worked exhaustively to make the sale. But it doesn't have to mean you've lost the business.

It's important to get to the heart of the matter first. While "our budget just got cut" might be the truth, it also can be code for another reason the buyer is backing away. And while it may feel like a final decision, often there's still room to negotiate. Use the LSCPA process from Chapter 3 to unearth the real problem:

- Listen closely to what the customer is saying. Was the budget cut specifically for this project, for example, or was there a reduction to the general department budget? The latter may provide additional room for negotiation
- Share your understanding of the situation.
- Clarify that the buyer still has a need to solve real problems identified in the Discovery stage. Those problems may even get worse should a purchase be delayed a year or two, costing more money in the long run.
- Problem solve to find additional ways to make the sale, perhaps with modifications that fit within the prospect's new financial parameters.

When money is the issue

If the issue truly is a lack of funds, these tactics can help in the problem-solving stage of LSCPA:

- Enlarge the circle of influencers. If you truly have a compelling story to tell, such as being able to save the prospect significant money in years one or two of implementation, you may not be preaching to the right people. You might need to work harder to reach the right influencers in the company. When you have testimonials, case studies or independent research data supporting your product, there's probably at least one analytical power broker in the prospect firm who'll see that spending money today could save or earn multiples of that investment down the line. Get them on your side, and you're on your way.

- Reassess needs. If money is indeed tighter, perhaps the prospect's market strategy has changed as well. Return to the Discovery stage and determine what those buying needs are today. Perhaps they don't need as much post-sale support. Perhaps they don't need your product today, but in six months to a year. Perhaps they need something else your company, or one of its subsidiaries, can provide.

- Gather intelligence. Is the prospect's retreat an isolated event or a sign that the whole industry is retrenching or reacting to a market downturn? The cutbacks may be related to the economy or part of an industry cycle you'll have to ride out. Your sales team may have to get creative to find solutions during this stretch.

Ask for the Sale

If your second round of Discovering makes it clear you can still help the company, put on your best Counselor salesperson demeanor and ask for the order despite the prospect's budget cutback. But keep these things in mind:

- Try a different closing technique. Use a balance sheet or a cost analysis tactic to show with hard numbers how your product or service can actually save the company money with the purchase. The impact will be double if you can point to similar clients who saved the same amount of money you're promising this prospect – and in the same time frame. Print multiple copies of these analyses so they can be distributed to key decision makers and purchase influencers.
- Offer flexible financing options. In today's companies sometimes

even a senior vice president can't even make a buying decision because the purse strings are held half a world away. If that's the case, work with your key decision makers to determine what they can do today, on their own authority. Offer flexible financing options that they can take to superiors. Perhaps money not available now might come free in the next few quarters.

- Empathize. Despite all your never-say-die hard work, sometimes the answer will still be no. While frustrating, it won't help to take it out on key contacts at the company. If the decision is indeed beyond their control, getting angry with them will only make matters worse. Instead, acknowledge that you understand there are no guarantees in the business world – and no hard feelings.

YOUR COMPANY MAY BE BOUGHT SOON

Situation:

After several years of fast growth and rising profits, your company has fallen on tough times. Analysts predict you may be ripe for a buyout. Unfortunately, as a salesperson, you still have quotas to make and you're wondering how to respond when customers say, "I'm not hearing the best things about your company right now."

Solution:

This is every salesperson's nightmare. You can dispel rumors and fight unfounded product slams, but when the cold hard truth is that your company is in trouble, how do you keep selling?

It's critical when you begin reading news stories or hearing word on the street that you get the official word from top executives. Request that they be candid with you. In addition to filling in the sales staff on the situation, top executives or sales managers also should prepare written materials for salespeople to give to their best customers.

If customers are curious, determine what they want to know about the situation. Perhaps they're only needling you to see how you will react. Maybe they're looking for reassurances that you will keep them apprised as things develop, especially if your prices rise, product is suddenly unavailable, support options change, or another development emerges that will affect their business. Maybe they don't care about your company as long as they know there will be continued support for the industrial equipment you sell. This is another good spot to reintroduce the LSPCA process by:

- Listening carefully to what the buyer is asking of you.
- Sharing your understanding of their concerns.
- Clarifying the buyer's real concerns.
- Problem solving by showing the buyer his options should the worst case happen.
- Asking for action from the buyer in the form of a commitment to continue buying from you until definitive news emerges.

Possible Responses

Depending on the situation, you can use several approaches with a customer who is asking if your company will still be in business next month. Among those tactics are:

- "Honestly, I don't know what the company will look like in a few months, but I do know that our core products will continue to have real advantages over the competition." This is a tactic that Silicon Graphics' sales force used when rumors of the company's demise began to surface in 2001.
- "I know we've been having a tough time of late, but you've probably also heard that we have some top-notch people working on it." This is what Apple Computer representatives said in the late 1990s when the company's stock plummeted to about US$1 a share. The board brought back co-founder Steve Jobs for his creativity, product development acumen, and ability to inspire the workforce.
- "We've had a lot of ups and downs in the 135 years we've been in business, but we've never, ever let a customer down. I personally

promise that I will not keep information from you and will do all that I can to assure that you get the service and support you need." This is the tactic venerable U.S. retailing giant Montgomery Ward used when it went out of business in the late 1990s. Most customers were given more than a year's warning about the closing.

YOUR CLIENT BUYS THROUGH A PURCHASING COMMITTEE

Situation:

A buying decision is delegated to a purchasing review committee without high disclosure about the group's buying criteria and little opportunity to find out who they are, much less interview them for your Discovering or Advocating work.

Solution:

There are two clear options in this case. One is to work around the system by tactfully building rapport with some members of the buying committee or their work associates. Another is to submit the required proposal so your name stays in the pool, but this does little to help you separate from the contenders.

Going Around

Circumventing the system is possible if you're done your homework and established the right relationships in the prospect company. Start by asking those contacts what they think the criteria will be. You may become enlightened very quickly. In the worst case, you'll have a few doors slammed in your face or "policy" cited as a reason contacts can provide no more than perfunctory or baseline information.

Large government institutions often use this process when making capital purchases, with the intention of keeping the buying process fair or abiding by regulatory bidding requirements. Yet this process tends to shortchange a vital component of the purchasing decision – the track record and post-purchase service support of the salesperson and his company. The salesperson, service contact, or installation team are the ones who will handle any problems with payment, installation, or product support. Their ability to handle deftly any problems or disputes in the post-sale environment is very important. You need to find acceptable ways to highlight your team's expertise.

Persuading decision makers or purchase influencers of this added capability can help you work around the established buying process and set yourself apart. Purchase influencers, those who counsel decision makers but don't have direct decision-making authority, are particularly valuable in this situation as conduits to information about bid objectives. In government settings, these influencers might be agency administrators and not, for example, the head of purchasing. The administrator understands what his or her department needs and knows how to help you position a sales proposal to stand out in the eyes of purchasing, as long as they're not defying policy or abandoning ethics in talking to you.

In for-profit companies, chief influencers are often department managers. They usually have a real stake in the outcome of a purchase decision and, since they're not on the "off-limits" purchasing committee, are easier to contact and persuade to support your product in their conversations with committee members. For example, if you can get these purchase influencers to embrace the benefits of intangible product features like 24-hour customer service support, they might relay the message to the committee. That may help redefine a request for proposal in your favor.

The Cattle Call

If you can't make inroads with purchase influencers or other contacts at the company, and the purchase process is moving swiftly, all you can do is opt for the low bid by filling out the buyer's request for proposal and hoping for the best. Even if you don't land a face-to-face meeting to illustrate why your product trumps the competition, it will keep your name in the file for the next purchasing cycle.

Follow Up

No matter which tactic you pursue, remember to follow up with some-one at the prospect company who's either a decision maker or pur-chase influencer. If you didn't get the business, ask why (if they're at liberty to say.) Ask what you might have done to position yourself more effectively. Ask what set the winner apart from the rest. Ask if you can call this person the next time there's a similar buying need.

You may not get helpful answers to any of these questions – or re-sponses at all – but if you do, it's likely to help considerably next time you face a similar situation.

YOUR CLIENT IS SETTING UP PREFERRED PROVIDERS

Situation:

Customers are trying to line you up in their "preferred provider" ma-chinery. You have to satisfy numerous requirements and give prospects all of your best prices, but without any guarantee that they will buy anything.

Solution:

This situation isn't as daunting as it appears. Most companies that use preferred providers choose only a few from any one industry. By being asked to satisfy the requirements, you've already made an important first cut. That improves your odds of getting onto a final preferred provider list and may put you on a list of suppliers some employees can choose to buy from immediately.

Preferred provider lists are increasingly common in large corpora-tions. They winnow the list of qualified vendors for given product cat-egories, simplifying and adding consistency to the internal purchasing process. Thus they ensure buyers receive volume discounts when product is bought at several locations or from different company divi-sions.

The good news is that, unlike a "blind" bidding process handled by a purchasing committee, there is ample opportunity for salespeople to build rapport with decision makers. Many preferred providers are chosen not just based on low price, but on a combination of factors including price, quality, reliability, delivery speed, service support, or even similar operating philosophies.

Common Questions

Some common questions buyers will ask in assessing your preferred provider worthiness are:

- What are your payment options?
- What volume-discount options are available?
- Do those discounts accrue on different products?
- What are your delivery, service support, and problem-resolution options?
- What are the specs on each of the products you provide?
- How long have you been doing business with us or our industry?
- What other companies do you supply, and how long have you supplied them?

These questions won't reveal any secrets. They're all queries you might answer during the four stage of the Counselor-selling process. What can help, however, is making sure all your answers are up to date. That will help you pull together accurate preferred provider proposals much faster.

YOUR CLIENT'S CEO AWARDS THE DEAL TO A FRIEND

Situation:

You have done business with a client for several years but the CEO recently decided to give your business to a friend of his who competes with you. The decision makers in the company – still strong supporters of yours – say their hands are tied.

Solution:

If may not be easy, but you need to take the "long view" here. Chances are the CEO's friend has the business locked in, barring a major lack of performance on his part, for at least a year or so. But the CEO won't be in power forever. And if the CEO's friend performs poorly, the board of directors will eventually hear about it.

Some tactics to use here are:

- Look for ways to distinguish your products and services. With some competitive reconnaissance you may be able to position your company as offering something the CEO's friend doesn't. Perhaps you sell industrial equipment. Maybe you didn't get the multimillion-dollar equipment account that went to the CEO's buddy, but your company also sells cleaning solvents for the equipment – something the friend's company doesn't offer. Not only might you land a good piece of business, it's a way of keeping your company's name in front of decision makers.

- Continue to build rapport in Counselor-salesperson fashion. If the CEO is fired in six months, you could be the first one called to bid against or replace his friend. And although the choice of the CEO's friend may be a foregone conclusion, the company may still undertake a formal purchasing process. If the CEO is closely involved in it, don't exclude him from your Relating and Discovering. You may sell to him again in a future position, and you want him to remember your professionalism and sales acumen.

- Work to educate the CEO on his options. Send the CEO articles or studies that may help him see the situation in a different light, but that don't appear to be undermining his friend. If the CEO is insisting on buying a mainframe computer system from a long-time colleague when everyone else in the industry is opting for application service providers (ASPs), an article summarizing the trend – and the benefit of ASPs versus other options – might open his eyes. This way the objective information or data does the selling for you.

- Never criticize the competition. If it gets back to the CEO that you are criticizing or sabotaging his friend, your chances of landing the business are probably over.

- Empathize and check in periodically. Chances are your contacts in the company are as frustrated by the CEO's decision as you are. You want to remain a good, loyal Counselor without criticizing the CEO's decision. Remind your contacts that you remain available to help or provide advice as needed, even if they have questions about dealing with the new supplier. Remember, not only do you want to stay in good stead with the company should the CEO leave or the new supplier not work out, you want to put yourself on the short list of potential suppliers should these decision makers themselves leave and be in a position to buy from you at a new company.

YOU SELL IN A DECLINING INDUSTRY

Situation:

You sell capital equipment to a declining industry. Experts say that many of your major clients won't exist in five to 10 years and that those who survive will be operating in vastly different ways.

Solution:

This is an all too common scenario in today's fast-changing global business environment. The companies or industries of today can disappear tomorrow, due to financial crisis, merger, technological advances, or even political events.

First, take a moment to congratulate yourself for recognizing the trend. It means you've performed your industry Discovery very well. You've diligently monitored the business and know what your customers may face in the future.

Is Your Company Ready?

In today's volatile markets, it's smart to assess the fit between your career aspirations and your company's strategic direction periodically.

Before setting foot in any prospect's office, you should know the following things about your own company:

- Are we constantly developing new products to meet customers' changing needs, or are we content to stay status quo?
- Have we adjusted to any long-term decline in sales to one industry by developing new products or strategies for selling into others?
- Are we poised to remain a leader in the industry?
- Are we seen as a consultant to the industry?

If you can't answer yes to these questions, you'll have a difficult time making sales if your major client industry begins a precipitous decline.

Be Innovative

No matter how well prepared your company is for a downturn, your job will grow infinitely more difficult if a crisis hits. Many of your customers will have reduced budgets for capital improvements, and some will be forced out of business. But if your company and sales managers support creative, flexible thinking in tough times, things may not be so bleak.

Consider the following approaches:

1. **Look for ways to sell current products into different industries.** Have you or any of your peers sold something that a customer put to a unique use? It may have seemed quirky at the time but could be a sign of a new market opportunity.
2. **Think creatively.** What basic needs does your capital equipment fulfill? Might other industries need those fundamentals? Could your equipment be modified slightly to meet needs in another market sector?
3. **Look for new ways to aid existing customers**. Are there other ways to help existing customers who can't afford capital upgrades, per-

haps by picking up a new line of products or offering services such as warehousing or just-in-time product delivery?

4. **Pursue ways to turn around negatives**. When the U.S. logging industry fell on hard times in the 1970s, large suppliers realized one contributing factor was a public perception that the industry was decimating the landscape. So the suppliers began working with industry associations to educate the public on the advantages of wood products and to show that selective logging can be good for the land. The effort contributed to a gradual but solid turnaround for the industry.

5. **Lend expertise to struggling customers**. The goal is to survive a downturn together with your clients. If your customers go out of business, it hurts you. In your Discovery work for clients, you probably noted some areas for improvement not directly related to your sale. Even if your company can't provide direct assistance, identify or pass along contacts or resources that can. If necessary, "loan out" your experts in areas such as finance, operations, or marketing for short periods to help your major clients keep their heads above water.

YOU SELL FOR THE FIRST TIME IN A NEW CULTURE

Situation:

Your company has just opened up new international sales offices in Germany, Mexico, and Singapore, and you've been reassigned to one of the offices. You're being asked to sell into a different culture, with different buying traditions and habits, for the first time.

Solution:

You've heard colorful stories about selling in the international marketplace. There's the sales rep who casually showed the sole of his shoe to an Arab businessmen during a meeting in Cairo and was asked not to return, the no-nonsense salesman in Mexico City who failed to do the appropriate relationship building before getting down to business, and the Western saleswoman in Japan who took the liberal use of "yes" in that culture to mean a deal was done, not as the intended meaning of "yes, I hear you."

Cultural awareness is essential to your success internationally, and you should give cross-cultural communication skills appropriate attention through reading or seminars, at the very least. Of course you also will need to be aware of the specific regional customs and traditions of business that apply wherever you do your business. The encouraging news is that as the world grows smaller and global business expands, people are more sophisticated, perhaps more tolerant of beginners, and in some cases, cultural differences are becoming less marked.

For starters, here are a few tips for making a smooth transition to selling to international markets:

1. **Find a mentor who's a cultural native.** A salesperson who's a native of the new country you're selling to can be an invaluable source of advice. Although it's helpful if this mentor works for your company or in your industry, it's not essential. You're looking for insight into the cultural norms of your new target market, the kind of counseling only an indigenous colleague can provide.

2. **Do your homework.** If you're dealing with a culture that doesn't allow women to close business deals, for example, you can still send your senior female salesperson to the closing meeting, but she should know not to take offense when the client directs questions to her junior male counterpart. Understanding these practices beforehand goes a long way toward avoiding any uncomfortable conflicts when you're face to face. And remember that while companies in a given area may share a common social culture, each organization has a corporate culture, and the people in that organization may be widely different from each other. This demands increased sensitivity on the Counselor salesperson's part at each stage of the selling process.

3. **Determine how you'll handle any ethical quandaries.** If bribery is an accepted part of doing business in the new country, you should know in advance how to handle it. Will your company view it as a cost of doing business or forbid it on ethical grounds? If it's forbidden, are there acceptable alternatives to a straight bribe, such as providing extra training or services, socializing, etc.?

4. **Look for common ground.** Depending on cultural preferences, it can help to concentrate on the personal aspects of building rapport in these situations. Finding common ground with customers can help build trust and overcome minor cultural differences. Check on the local customs, and then touch on acceptable non-business topics before you get down to business. But remember that some cultures prefer only a minimum of small talk before moving to business.

5. **Remember that most mistakes aren't fatal.** Many of your prospects have been in your shoes, and understand the nervousness that accompanies selling into new markets. While you might make a mistake, if it's not grievous, chances are it will quickly be forgiven with the proper apology and show of humility.

6. **Above all, check your arrogance at the door.** While you may not understand why a business culture works the way it does, the reality is you have to work within that system. Remain humble and respectful. Nothing will sink an international sale faster than a perception that you're trying to impose your cultural norms on a prospective buyer. When in serious doubt, ask what you should do next.

IF YOU'D LIKE TO LEARN MORE
ABOUT COUNSELOR SELLING SKILLS

Wilson Learning began offering Sales Sonics, the predecessor to *The Counselor Salesperson* program, in 1965. To date, more than a million participants around the world have learned the Counselor mindset and skills presented in this program, in both classroom and e-learning environments.

Organizations of all sizes and in a wide range of business and non-profit sectors use this program. Culturally adapted translations and custom versions for salespeople are available in 19 dialects and languages. Custom versions for salespeople and sales managers in the pharmaceutical, health care, retail, travel and leisure, automotive, high tech, IT, manufacturing, financial, insurance, capital equipment and other industries are also available. Find out more by visiting www.wilsonlearning.com.

"Wilson Learning played a critical role in the reinvention of our sales force and our clients' perception of our value."

Ron DeLio, Chief Operating Officer,
Strategic Travel Solutions Division, Rosenbluth International

"We've used the Counselor method for more than 20 years and have thousands of graduates of the course. Our mission is 'To be the best in the eyes of our customers, employees and shareholders,' which means 'Do what's right,' 'Do the best you can,' and 'Help customers, employees and shareholders get what they want.' The Counselor method has been and continues to be the CORE of our way of accomplishing our mission."

Ed Gilbertson, Manager, Sales & Management Training, TRANE,
An American Standard Company

"These Wilson Learning methods are 'how we do business.' They are what sets us apart from our competitors and the reason why our customers rate us more highly in customer satisfaction than our peers. In the Counselor method we have discovered the sales system solution that delivers on our customers' needs."

Paul Bryant, Senior Manager,
Financial Services, Suncorp Metway Ltd.

Win-Win Selling (ISBN Revised Edition 978-90-88720-01-7, Third Edition, 978-90-77256-34-3) 160 pages, softcover, with models, charts, anecdotes, index and resource lists. US$18.95, € 18.95

IF YOU'D LIKE TO LEARN MORE ABOUT VERSATILE SELLING SKILLS

Managing Interpersonal Relations, the program that pioneered Versatility techniques, was developed by Wilson Learning in the early 1970s. Ongoing refinement has led to the current program, *The Versatile Salesperson*. With more than a million graduates worldwide, Versatility is a proven asset to any sales process.

The Versatile Salesperson is available for both classroom and e-learning environments. A suite of tools supports ongoing learning with specialized planning checklists, advisory guidelines, a manager's tool kit, a CD-ROM reinforcement program, and other resources. A specially adapted version for the pharmaceutical industry, *The Versatile Pharmaceutical Representative*, is also available.

The program is used by organizations of all sizes and in a wide range of business and non-profit sectors. Culturally adapted translations are available in 19 dialects and languages. In addition to the pharmaceutical industry program, custom versions for salespeople and sales managers in the health care, retail, travel and leisure, automotive, high tech, IT, manufacturing, financial, insurance, capital equipment and other industries are also available. Find out more about *The Versatile Salesperson* and Wilson Learning locations by visiting www.wilsonlearning.com.

"If there is one factor that differentiates high performing salespeople, it is Versatility – the ability to adapt one's approach and style of communication to meet the personal needs and expectations of the customer. Every salesperson will acknowledge that their selling skills work better with some customers than with others. The skills in The Versatile Salesperson *help salespeople adapt to all types of customers and help ensure success."*

Ron Remillard, Director of the Sales Training and Development Institute,
Georgia Pacific Corporation

"The concepts in Versatile Selling changed my career and my life. I've been through a lot of training, and even after 33 years in sales I try to keep learning. Social Styles, Versatility and the Wilson Learning approach to sales have given me the solid foundation I needed to achieve the success that I've had.

W. Jacques Gibbs, Investment Advisor

Versatile Selling (ISBN 978-90-77256-03-9, Revised Edition 978-90-77256-35-0)
160 pages, softcover, with models, charts, anecdotes, index and resource lists.
US$18.95, € 18.95

Contributors

ABOUT THE AUTHORS

Tom Kramlinger, Ph.D., was a Senior Design Consultant at Wilson Learning. During more than 30 years with the company, he designed programs in sales and sales management and researched and designed special applications for clients in the capital equipment, financial, automotive, transport, chemical, IT, insurance and telecommunication industries. He taught *The Counselor Salesperson* pilot program in Japan and collaborated on its cultural adaptation there. His passion was creating and communicating advanced solutions for Fortune 500 global clients that integrate Wilson Learning technologies.

Michael Leimbach, Ph.D., is Vice President, Global Research and Development at Wilson Learning. He and his Global R&D team have created the innovative performance improvement systems that make Wilson Learning a leader in human performance improvement. He has been helping organizations gain sales force effectiveness for over 20 years. Michael has been involved with updating and enhancing all of Wilson Learning's sales-effectiveness programs and created Wilson Learning's sales-effectiveness diagnostic capabilities. He has published numerous professional articles and has presented before a wide range of clients and professional organizations around the world.

Ed Tittel, B.A., M.A., was a Senior Performance Consultant for Wilson Learning Worldwide. Ed had over 20 years' experience in the human performance improvement industry and co-authored several Wilson

Learning brand and custom offerings. During his tenure at Wilson Learning, he consulted with Fortune 100 organizations throughout the United States, Europe and Asia. Prior to his work at Wilson Learning, Ed was a developer and demonstrator for the National Diffusion Network within the United States Department of Education.

David Yesford is the Vice President, Product Marketing for Wilson Learning Worldwide. He has spent 17 years helping organizations develop an understanding of effective consultative sales strategies. David has been involved with creating, updating and customizing sales effectiveness systems and most recently has lead Wilson Learning's effort to launch blended sales effectiveness capabilities. David's primary interest is to ensure that a person's performance improves in ways he or she values and the organization needs.

ABOUT THE PROJECT DEVELOPMENT TEAM

Brian McDermott is a consultant, business writer and editor with extensive experience in the field, particularly in the area of training.
Karien Sticker is a graphics designer specialized in instructional page design.
Wouter Geukens is a graphics designer specializing in books.
Andrew Karre is an editor and book designer.

All the authors at Wilson Learning and the Nova Vista Publishing staff wish to thank the team, and others who lent their expertise, for their enthusiasm, dedication and resourcefulness in developing this book.

Index

A
Account penetration, 125
Advantage, 14-17
Advocating, 10, 20, 63-111, 118-119, 124-125, 144
Ask for the order, 92, 96-97
Assumptive close, 91-93, 96, 102
  balance sheet, 93
  cost analysis, 94
  mini-max, 93
  next step, 94
  options, 94
  summing up, 94

B
Back wheel knowledge, 65
Ben Duffy approach, 33-36
Benefit, 33, 70-72, 118
  gaining, 71
  maintaining, 71-72
Best interest of customer, 36
Bicycle analogy, 65-66, 110
Blame, 75, 121
Broll, Jan, 40
Buyer roles, 20
  budget director, 78-79
  concept, 77, 79
  economic, 76-77, 79
  end user, 78-79
  feasibility, 77-79
    gatekeeper, 76-77
    multiple roles, 78-79
Buyer's remorse, 20, 112-13, 117
Buying motives, see Purchase motivation
Business problem, 17, 19

C
Carey, Pat, 66, 97, 110-11
Case studies, 20-21, 130-153
Catchers, 43
Cattle call, 145
Checking questions, 72
Closing, 25, 63, 90, 94, 110, 141; see also

Assumptive close
Commonality, 25, 28-29, 31-32, 153
Communication, 84-90
  abstract words, 85
  analogies, 86
  compare/contrast, 87
  drama, 88
  "feel" the benefit, 85
  prospect's language, 85
  show vs. tell, 86
Competence, 27-28, 31, 32, 37, 65, 81, 133
Competitive intelligence, 83-84, 141
Complex objections, 102-109; see also Objections
Complaints, 90, 100, 112
"Consultative selling," 43
Counselor
  approach, 11, 13, 18, 20-21, 39
  evolution, 16-17
  mindset, 11, 18, 21, 119
  sales, 13, 16, 18-21, 29, 32, 34, 38, 39, 64, 69, 97, 128, 130, 135, 141, 148, 152
  selling strategies, 130
Credibility, 25-26, 35, 75, 81, 132, 137
Cross-cultural sales, 151-153
Customer as advocate, see Internal advocates

D
Differentiation, 40, 67, 148
Discovery Agreement, 43-49, 54, 56, 70, 72, 74-75, 81-82, 90, 91, 94, 96, 100, 103
  sample, 46
Discovery faux pas, 54-56
Discovery, 10, 19-20, 37-62, 64, 70, 72-75, 81-82, 90-91, 94, 96-97, 100, 103, 107, 112, 124-126, 132, 134, 140-141, 144, 148-151; see also Listening, Questioning
Dissatisfaction, 10, 114-16
Documentation, 82

E
Edison, Thomas, 95
E-mail, 139
Empathy, 33-35, 142
Enhancing the relationship, 125-29
Eras in selling, 14-17
Esatisfy.com, 116

Evolution of practice of selling, 13-17

F
Fact-finding questions, 47, 49, 132
Fear, in customer, 113-114, 118
Fear, in salesperson, 94-97
Feeling-finding questions, 48-49
Four obstacles to buying, 18-20; see also Obstacles to buying
Four pillars of support, 116-29
Friedman, Jackie, 69
Front wheel skills, 65
Fry, Art 63
Fulfillment, performance with, 8-9, 11-13, 21

G
Gap between Have and Want, 43-45
Gatekeepers, 76-77, 137
Golden Rule, 39
Goodyear Corporation, 129
Gove, Bill, 43
Government institutions, 144-46

H
Handling dissatisfaction, 121-25
Have(s), 43-45
Helms, Nick, 46
Hidden influencers, 54

I
IBM, 110-111
Implementation, 10, 20, 116, 120
Indifference, 114
Influences, external, 61-62
Influences, internal, 60-61
Influencers, 47, 54, 60, 61, 76, 140
Internal advocates, 80-81
Intent, 10, 19, 25, 30
Isotec, 42

K
Kramlinger, Tom, 41, 156

L
Leimbach, Michael, 156
Listening, 39, 50-52
Loss leader, 15, 136

LSCPA Model (Listen-Share-Clarify-Problem Solve-Action), 96-102, 121, 140, 143
Luce, Don, 117-18, 121

M
Mackay, Harvey, 82
Managing the implementation, 120-21
Mayo Clinic, 42
Medtronic, 99-100
Motives and appeals, 20, 40, 57, 60, 107
Motives, personal, see Personal agenda or motive
Multime Company, 129

N
National Cash Register, 129
Need(s), 10-11, 16-21, 42-43, 47, 64, 71, 139-40
Needs-based selling, 15, 38
Needs survey, 124
No help, no need, no satisfaction, no trust, see Obstacles to buying
"No Hurry" phenomenon, 113-114
Non-profit, 135

O
Objections, 90, 96-109
Obstacles to buying, 18-20
   no trust, 10, 18-19, 22-36
   no need, 10, 18-19, 37-62
   no help, 10, 18, 20, 41, 63-111
   no satisfaction, 10, 20, 112-120

P
Partnership with customers, 10, 16, 20, 43
Performance with fulfillment, 8-9, 11-13, 21
Personal agenda or motive, 76, 103, 106-09
   approval, 108
   power, 107
   recognition, 107-08
   respect, 109
Pitch, 43, 80
Plan B, 82
Positioning, 83

Preferred provider, 146-47
Presentation, 39, 55, 63, 74, 80, 102
Price, 97, 107, 130-131, 135-137, 147,
Problems, problem solving attitude, 10,
    19, 38-42, 68, 97, 99, 103, 110
Product knowledge, 65-66
Propriety, 25-27, 31-32, 133
Purchase influencers, 47, 52-54, 74, 119,
    134, 145
Purchase motivation, 20, 44, 56-60, 113
    task motives, 57-58
    personal motives, 57-60
Purchase roles, 53
Purchasing committee, 144
Purpose, process, payoff (3 Ps), 32-33, 36,
    131, 133

Q
Questioning techniques, 33-35, 39, 45-50
    best/least, 48
    catch-All, 50
    checking, 51
    fact-finding, 47-49,52
    feeling-finding, 48, 52
    magic wand, 50
    permission, 47

R
Relating, 10, 19, 22-36, 64, 96, 112, 125,
    131, 134, 148
Relationship tension, 23-25, 33, 47
Riddell, Tevilla, 117

S
Saab, 117
SAB (Solution Advantage Benefit), 70-
    72, 74, 76, 91
Sabre, 68-70
Sale botched, 41
Satisfaction, 71, 110, 114-16
Shapiro, George, 84
Silver, Spenser, 63
Smythe, Jonathan, 99-100
Soft skills, 65
Solutions, 16
Sondrall, Keith, 67, 98, 100, 102, 115
St. George, Fred, 129
Stalling, 112-13

Strategies, 15, 79
Supporting, 10, 20, 112-129
Supporting the buying decision, 117-19
Sustainable advantage, 10
Switching costs, 17

T
Task agenda, 76, 103
    operational justification, 103
    financial justification, 103
Task fears, 113
Task tension 19, 24-25, 79, 92
Third parties, 29, 87-89
Thompson, John, 129
3M Corporation, 63
3 Ps see Purpose, Process, Payoff
Time/tension model, 24
Tittel, Ed, 156-57
Trust, 10, 19, 21, 21-25, 29 102

U
University of Minnesota, 84

V
Value adding, 32, 97, 126-29, 135

W
Want(s), 11, 21, 43-45
Whistle presentation, 67-68, 70
Williams, Bill, 129
Win-win, 10, 21, 30, 110
Wilson, Larry, 8-9, 16, 95-96
Wilson Learning Corporation, Wilson
    Learning Worldwide, 11, 16, 21, 25, 29,
    40, 67, 95, 115, 117

Y
Yesford, David, 157

Z
Zone of indifference, 114-16

OTHER TITLES IN THE WILSON LEARNING LIBRARY

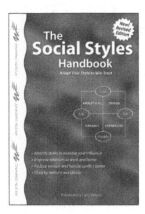

Social Styles Handbook: Adapt Your Style to Win Trust

Backed by a database of more than 2 million people, Wilson Learning's Social Styles concepts are powerful, life-changing communication tools. The ways people prefer to influence others and how they feel about showing emotion identify them as Analyticals, Expressives, Drivers or Amiables. You feel comfortable acting within your own style. But to relate to others well, you must consciously adjust your style to theirs. That's Versatility, which improves performance in every aspect of your work and life.

Find your style and learn to recognize others'. Understand and appreciate the strengths and differences in each. Learn how to become Versatile while still being yourself. Important tools for recognizing tension and Back-Up Behavior and handling it productively, plus techniques for influencing others, have made this a best-selling book that delivers results.

"I'm not sure I can quantify the value of using Social Styles, but I know I would not want to do my job without it."

Ann Horner, Main Board Director,
Bourne Leisure Limited

Social Styles Handbook (ISBN Revised Edition 978-90-77256-33-6)
192 pages, 160 X 230 cm (6" x 9")
Suggested retail price: € 19.95, US$19.95
Models, charts, anecdotes, an index and other resources.

Versatile Selling: Selling the Way Your Customer Wants to Buy.

This book presents the concepts and tools of *The Social Styles Handbook*, specifically adapted for the needs of salespeople. The powerful yet simple skill of Versatility – the ability to read and adapt to the natural behavior of your customers – makes them feel comfortable and ready to buy, and has been proven to increase sales measurably. Learn to assess your own Social Style (Driver, Analytical, Amiable, or Expressive) and the style of your customer. That way you know how your customer wants to be treated, and you can adapt your own behavior to the customer's specific needs and expectations. You will also know how to respond to and decrease unproductive tension and get back to productive collaboration, because you know how to handle Back-Up Behaviors of customers of different styles. No matter what sales process you use, this book will help you work better with every customer.

"The concepts in Versatile Selling changed my career and my life. I've been through a lot of training, and even after 33 years in sales I try to keep learning. Social Styles, Versatility and the Wilson Learning approach to sales have given me the solid foundation I needed to achieve the success I've had."

W. Jacques Gibbs, Investment Advisor

Versatile Selling (ISBN 978-90-77256-03-9, Revised Edition 978-90-77256-35-0)
160 pages, 160 X 230 cm (6" x 9")
Suggested retail price: € 18.95, US$18.95
Models, charts, anecdotes, an index and other resources.

CAREERS

I Just Love My Job!
Roy Calvert, Brian Durkin, Eugenio Grandi and Kevin Martin, in the Quarto Consulting Library (ISBN 978-90-77256-02-2, softcover, 192 pages, $19.95)

Taking Charge of Your Career
Leigh Bailey (ISBN 978-90-77256-13-8, softcover, 96 pages, $14.95)

LEADERSHIP AND INNOVATION

Grown-Up Leadership
Leigh Bailey and Maureen Bailey (ISBN 978-90-77256-09-1, softcover, 144 pages, $18.95)

Grown-Up Leadership Workbook
Leigh Bailey (ISBN 978-90-77256-15-2, softcover, 96 pages, $14.95)

Leading Innovation
Brian McDermott and Gerry Sexton (ISBN 978-90-77256-05-3, softcover, 160 pages, $18.95)

Time Out for Leaders
Donald Luce and Brian McDermott (ISBN 978-90-77256-10-7, hardcover with marker ribbon, $19.95; ISBN 978-90-77256-30-5, softcover, $14.95)

SALES

Time Out for Salespeople
Nova Vista Publishing's Best Practices Editors (ISBN 978-90-77256-14-5, hardcover with marker ribbon, 272 pages, $19.95; ISBN 978-90-77256-31-2, softcover, 272 pages, $14.95)

Get-Real Selling, Revised Edition
Michael Boland and Keith Hawk (ISBN 978-90-77256-32-9, softcover, 144 pages, $18.95)

CUSTOMER SERVICE AND ORGANIZATIONAL TRANSFORMATION

Service Excellence @ Novell
Nova Vista Publishing's Best Practices Editors (ISBN 978-90-77256-11-4, softcover, 112 pages, $18.95)

SCIENCE PARKS, ECONOMICS, ECOLOGY OF INNOVATION

What Makes Silicon Valley Tick?
Tapan Munroe, Ph.D., with Mark Westwind, MPA (ISBN 978-90-77256-28-2, softcover, 192 pages, $19.95)

See previous page for Wilson Learning Library titles.

Visit **www.novavistapub.com** for sample chapters, reviews, links and ordering.